·BARBERTON·
FRIED CHICKEN

·BARBERTON·
FRIED CHICKEN
An Ohio Original

RONALD KOLTNOW

AMERICAN PALATE

Published by American Palate
A Division of The History Press
Charleston, SC
www.historypress.com

Front cover, top: images courtesy of James Carney; *bottom*: courtesy of the *Akron Beacon Journal.*
Back cover, top: courtesy of James Carney; *bottom*: courtesy of the author.

First published 2018

Manufactured in the United States

ISBN 9781467139724

Library of Congress Control Number: 2018948040

"Why did the chicken cross the road?
It was trying to escape from Barberton."

—From the Chickenfest joke contest, 1989,
quoted by Stuart Warner in the *Akron Beacon Journal*

Dedicated to the late Mark H. Koltnow, DPM, and the late Jeffrey M. Katz, the two biggest Barberton fried chicken fans I ever knew, and dedicated to the love of my life, Barbara L. Trainer, upon whose strength I rely.

CONTENTS

ACKNOWLEDGEMENTS

The great Beach Boy and amateur philosopher Brian Wilson wrote a song called "It Takes a Mess of Help to Stand Alone." Truer words were never spoken. First, thanks to all of those who shared Barberton fried chicken dinners with me, most of whom I love: Carl Bonner, Katie Byard, Jim Carney, Robert Hoffman, Chuck Johnston, Harold Koltnow, Wanda Koltnow, Gretchen Laatsch, James D. Switzer and David Weiner. Jim Switzer, by the way, was a member of the tasting committee for the Great Barberton Chick-Off in 1983.

The restaurant owners, and family members, were the most valuable of resources. Deep gratitude and respect for Kosta Papich and his son Milos Papich (and his wife, Maja) of Belgrade Gardens, Brian Canale of Hopocan Gardens and White House Chicken, Rikki Milich Neubecker of Milich's Village Inn, Sue Macko Cianciola of the Macko family and the new kid on the block, Scott Marble of Village Inn Chicken. Extra thanks go to the restaurant employees who spoke to a traveling scholar—Glen "Cookie" Cook, formerly of Village Inn; Debi Merl at White House Chicken; Melinda Waller at Belgrade Gardens; and so many others.

Many Barbertonians, Akronites and former residents of the area shared personal stories and reminiscences of Barberton and Barberton fried chicken. There are too many to list, although some of them are mentioned in the text. Big thanks go out to all who responded in person, via e-mail or on the "Akron, Ohio Memories" and "Barberton Fried Chicken" Facebook pages. Thank you all, people of home.

ACKNOWLEDGEMENTS

Norma Hill and Kim Barth of the *Akron Beacon Journal* provided photographs and insight into my research. Michael G. Kindness offered friendship and books to aid the project.

The world is a richer place with librarians in it. Many hardworking research librarians guided my studies, sent me photos, answered questions big and small and found valuable resources for me. My heartfelt gratitude to Sarah Hays of the Barberton Public Library (the local history room there is a treasure-trove, a model of its type) and to Mary Plazo, Rebecca Larson-Troyer and Barbara Leden of the Akron Summit County Public Library. An additional thank-you to the Akron Public Library's Bob Ethington, head of the popular culture department, who did not help with the research but who is a nice boy.

The aforementioned Katie Byard and Jim Carney are associated with the *Akron Beacon Journal*. Katie writes the weekly Akron Dish column. She has given support and guidance and has served as facilitator and ad hoc research assistant. She has been generous with her time, her knowledge, her books and her husband. Jim Carney, now retired from the *Beacon*, was my sounding board and photographer. Together, this couple was the best resource a boy could have. Thanks also to the *Beacon*'s Lisa Abraham, Paula Schleis and Jane Snow, who paved the way with their articles.

If every city had a mayor as charismatic and as accessible as Barberton's William B. Judge, urban areas would be as vibrant as Barberton is now. Bill, as he likes to be called, takes great pride in his city and is willing to talk about it. Thank you for your time, Mr. Mayor.

Many residents of Barberton, from restaurant owners to private citizens, made my job easier. Alberta and Eugene Bonner made me a home-cooked dinner and showed me the wonders of regional cuisine. (It was the first time that I had eaten squirrel.) Gary and Rhonda Ziegenhorn at the Erie Depot took time from a family celebration to talk about the history of the place. (They have great ice cream, too.) Adam and Marie Reinhardt of Ignite Brewery are breathing new life into downtown Barberton. Thanks also to John Kriston of the Green Diamond Grille for the *palascintas*.

A scholar walks in the footsteps of those who went before. Food writers John T. Edge, Emelyn Rude and Jan and Michael Stern gave me encouragement, and some even share my enthusiasm for Barberton fried chicken. Edge's book *Fried Chicken: An American Story* had the approach I tried to emulate in this book, a focus on the food and the personalities of those involved. The patron saint of this book, though, is Phyllis Taylor, the Barberton history specialist. Ms. Taylor wrote the Talk of the Town column in the *Barberton Herald* and is the author of a couple of highly informative books of local history. Her association with the Barberton Public Library puts her in great stead (see my love of librarians earlier). Whenever I had questions, I could generally find answers in Taylor's books. I have never met Ms. Taylor but am deeply indebted to her. She truly deserves her star on Barberton's Walk of Fame.

A writer needs many goads, people who give encouragement and argue against going to the movies on a work day. My wife, Barbara, was in the forefront. An angel in human form, Barbara understands why fried chicken is so important to me. My friends, including the team of Carney and Byard, stood behind me and pushed me forward: Alex Beam, Robert Birnbaum, Carl Bonner, Dan E. Moldea, Robert Segedy, Jim Switzer, David C. Taylor and my cousin Fred S. Vigder (who ate Barberton chicken after hearing me speak about it) gave encouragement, shared passion and lighted the path for a debut writer. Laura Hillenbrand is my heroine and has guided me by example. She is a great historian and a fine writer—and a lover of animals as well. WAKR-AM's Bobbi Horvath and, once again, Jim Carney, had me on their show to do some pre-publicity gabbing about chicken. Anne Whalen, bookseller extraordinaire, gave the manuscript a thorough reading. Any remaining errors are mine alone (in which case, I should have listened to her).

Wikipedia, the online encyclopedia, contains information on everything from Barberton fried chicken to match manufacturing to biographies of key players of American history. I owe it much and donate frequently. If you feel like it, use and support this valuable resource. Please consider joining me in donating to Wikipedia (donate@wikimedia.org).

Acquisitions Editor John Rodrigue of The History Press immediately shared the excitement I felt for fried chicken and encouraged me, assisted me and saw this book into print. Thank you for offering me the opportunity. Thanks to Katie Parry in sales, Sarah Haynes in publicity, master editor Rick Delaney and everyone at The History Press for enabling historians, amateur and otherwise, to publish specialized stories of regional appeal. Again, see comments about editing and all remaining errors being my own.

Lastly, thank you to the chickens who have given their lives on our behalf. As an animal lover, I am always trying to reconcile my carnivorous lifestyle with my love of our animal friends. When we eat Barberton chicken, we should be aware that these birds gave their lives to make us happy. There are those who say, "Love Your Animals, Don't Eat Them." I say, if you eat meat, eat it mindfully. Thank them for their sacrifice and appreciate that the circle of life sometimes is not pretty. Chickens can be beautiful, in the yard or on the plate. Farms like Gerber's raise their poultry with decency and process them as humanely as possible. I will not be hypocritical about eating animals. They die for our enjoyment; the least we can do is acknowledge the joy they give us.

I happen to love fried chicken and hope that you do, too.

FRIED CHICKEN: AN APPRECIATION

What's more, fried chicken is the stuff of song.
—*John T. Edge,* Fried Chicken: An American Story

Expertly fried chicken makes a noise when you bite into it. It can be described as a hearty crunch, as the teeth penetrate the golden crust. But perhaps *snap* is the better word. It is the breaking of a seal, if the breading has bonded perfectly with the chicken. The diner should hear that sound to be assured that the bird has been prepared to the highest level to which a fried chicken can aspire. The crust should, at first glance, be uniformly golden brown, perhaps with a tinge of bronze. When the seal is broken by that first bite, the hot juices, not to be confused with grease, should flow, hot and luxuriously. If there is no flowing juice, just dry meat, the bird has failed the test. There might be steam, but eating it fresh is worth the heat. The taste should be primarily of fowl. There are those who find chickens bland, and there are others who bury the flavor with herbs and spices. They are wrong. The best fried chicken chefs allow the subtlety of the bird to speak for itself.

Fried chicken has been a beloved American dish for decades. It is generally regarded as a southern dish, although many cultures brought their methods of frying chicken to these shores. The Bon Chon chain, and other local practitioners, have made the world aware of Korean fried chicken. Even Philadelphia's Federal Doughnut chain serves Korean fried chicken. The Chinese had been sautéing chickens, generally coated in a flour or herb blend, in woks for centuries before African slaves in the American South are said to have perfected the recipe. Reay Tannahill, in her *Food in History*, states that the Chinese had been preparing chicken since the second century. When the Mughal Empire was established in India in the sixteenth century, it brought its chicken recipes from Persia. (Curried chicken may not be what we think of as fried chicken, but it is first fried before it is sauced.) In the Middle Ages, fritters were a common dish—yeasty bits of dough fried with meat or fruit inside. Some of that meat was, for the purposes of this argument, chicken. Tom Nealon writes in his *Food Fights & Culture Wars: A Secret History of Taste* that a medieval recipe involved removing chicken from its bone, "the bone cleaned and boiled, and, finally, the chicken rewrapped around the bone and fried." In short, it was a processed dish made to look like fried chicken.

Many food historians believe that what we consider the traditional fried chicken had its roots in Scottish cooking—the Scots were the first to deep-fry chicken in boiling fat. Still, it is considered an American dish, especially a dish of the American South. Perhaps it is the Scots-Irish immigration to the southern states in the seventeenth century and the arrival of slaves—who brought with them their traditional African cooking methods—that gave fried chicken its foothold in that region.

There are fried chicken recipes that date to Roman times. In the fourth-century cookbook *Apicius*, attributed to the otherwise unknown Caelius Apicius, there is a recipe for *pullum frontonianum*, a chicken dish fried and later baked with fruit and herbs. Tannahill states that domestic hens were common in ancient Rome, invaluable for their eggs and for sacrifices, and even mentions a recipe for fowl drowned in wine. The Austro-Hungarian Empire gave us *pahovana piletina* and *wiener backhendl*, which would evolve somewhat into Barberton fried chicken, of which more later.

Still, we think of fried chicken as being a dish of the American South. The purpose of this book is to change the focus back to the European origins of fried chicken and to study the fried chicken that immigrants, especially those from Eastern Europe, brought with them as a reminder of what they left behind. Jeff Smith writes in his book *The Frugal Gourmet on Our Immigrant Ancestors* that immigrants "know it's terribly important to retain those characteristics of our immigrant ancestry, characteristics that will help us remember who we are." Is there any characteristic that defines a group more than their home-style cooking? John T. Edge, director of the Southern Foodways Alliance and award-winning food writer, opens his book *Fried Chicken: An American Story* with a dismissal of the southern hegemony on fried chicken. He writes: "Fried chicken is best served without a side of provincial bluster." When the Food Network featured Barberton fried chicken on its *Food Feuds* program, the host said that Barberton's "one-of-a-kind style... shows the South who's boss."

There are many regional fried chicken specialties to be found across the United States, from New England berched chicken to Hawaiian mochiko breaded wings. Barberton fried chicken, sometimes referred to as Serbian fried chicken, is the quintessential dish for the people of Northeastern Ohio.

This book will study fried chicken and its many practitioners. It will trace the history of the city of Barberton, its ups, its downs and its reinvention. It will discuss the city's founder, Ohio Columbus Barber, who was a visionary and an innovator. Finally, it will discuss Barberton's famous chicken houses—the key four are Belgrade Gardens, Hopocan Gardens, the White House and Village Inn Chicken (formerly Milich's Village Inn). Terrace Gardens and Macko's Restaurant also were part of the tradition but are now defunct. The four existing chicken houses, and a handful of other Eastern European specialists in the area, had a profound effect on the culture of this working-class suburb of Akron, Ohio.

Barberton fried chicken provided jobs (the current mayor of the city started at Belgrade Gardens as a busboy) and a livelihood for many immigrant families. Brian Canale of Hopocan Gardens and White House Chicken said that, together, the chicken houses are one of the top five employers in the city. If you grew up in Barberton, he said, chances are good that your first job was at a fried chicken house. The chicken houses brought a touch of home to the Eastern Europeans of the city. It also became part of family rituals, the place for Sunday dinners, holiday gatherings and wedding receptions. On Mother's Day in 1969, the five existing chicken houses served more than twenty-five thousand dinners (in a city of thirty-six thousand). Members of the Akron diaspora still flock to Barberton whenever they return home, and the Barberton faithful can still be seen at the restaurants after church on Sundays. In days when the mails allowed such things, the restaurants would ship dinners to chicken fans across the states and even to soldiers stationed in Vietnam.

The Serbian fried chicken houses were profiled on the cover of the *Akron Beacon Journal Magazine* in 1978. The cover of the magazine declared "It's Sunday in Barberton: Welcome to Chicken City." Times change, but fried chicken does not. At the four Barberton chicken houses, it is more than a matter of turning out great fried chicken dinners; it is a tradition that needs to be scrupulously upheld and respected.

Chapter One

A BRIEF, BUT LIVELY, HISTORY OF BARBERTON

PART 1: THE CITY

O.C. Barber, the millionaire of parlor-match fame, is going to build a manufacturing town bearing his name, which will depend for prosperity on industries conducted by his capital. He has already had the name of New Portage changed to Barberton and within the last two weeks three large companies, all with O.C. Barber at their head, have been organized to do business in the new town.
—New York Times, *October 5, 1891*

In many ways, the history of Barberton, Ohio, is no different than that of any northern industrial city—Gary, Indiana; Erie, Pennsylvania; or any other once vibrant industrial center you can name. Barberton, a city of 9.26 square miles, is located to the southwest of Akron, another former industrial center hit hard in the latter part of the twentieth century. These cities started small, generally as farmland. During the Industrial Revolution, and as our republic entered the twentieth century, with its wars and territorial expansion, the northern industrial cities grew prosperous and vital. Then, later in the century, times—and economic assumptions—changed. Manufacturing became stagnant. Jobs went to the American South or to Mexico or even abroad. The industrial city, where workers were able to earn enough to enter the middle class, was hit by job loss and straitened circumstances. Barberton,

Barberton in 1941, an industrial town and home of Serbian fried chicken, an Ohio original. *Photo courtesy of the Akron Beacon Journal.*

though, has a strong civic pride and identity and a shared cultural heritage (although the population is made up of many separate cultures). This has helped the city, and its famed fried chicken restaurants, as it goes through the process of revitalization.

Anyone who has ever spent a winter in Barberton would be surprised to learn that it had once been, 300 million years ago, a tropical area with dense vegetation. The original residents of Barberton lived in Connecticut, although few would think of it that way. The area where Barberton is situated was a part of the Western Reserve, an area claimed in the eighteenth century by the colony of Connecticut. Following the Treaty of Greenville in 1795, in which native tribes ceded land to the European settlers, the region became part of the Northwest Territory. It was considered the frontier, the westernmost part of the United States. The motto of the territory was "Meliorem lapsa locavi" (He has planted one better than the one fallen).

As is usually the case with lands considered frontier by the European settlers, the Northwest Territory did have indigenous residents, who were not considered honorary residents of Connecticut. The Lenape people, whom the colonists called the Delaware, moved farther west after suffering at the hands of rival tribes and from European-imported diseases. The tribe's name was *Lenni Lenape*, which translates roughly to "original man." They may not have been the original residents of the area, but that is where the history begins. The Lenape were matrilineal, which places the mother's clan in primary importance in establishing kinship and identity. This was not common with other tribes. Their society was divided into three major groups, or phratries, if you want to sound anthropological. *Phratry*, by the way, has the same root as "fraternity." Each phratry was divided into clans, as many as twelve clans per group.

Konieschquanoheel (Maker of Daylight) was a chief of the Wolf clan in the area surrounding what we now call Barberton. More commonly known as Chief Hopocan, he led his people along the portage path between the Cuyahoga and Tuscarawas Rivers. Their portage originally took them near the site that would become Belgrade Gardens, the primogenitor of Barberton fried chicken. They settled at the Portage. Later, the Lenape moved their settlement farther west, into an area that would be named New Portage. Hopocan called himself the King of New Portage. A statue of Chief Hopocan now greets visitors who travel from the old portage to the new. He stands on the corner of Wooster Road and Norton Avenue in New Portage Park. The statue was dedicated by Mayor William Mitchell in 1911. Its cost was originally $245, but the city ponied up the extra $38 for a bronze coating. The statue, designed by James B. Clow & Sons of Chicago and built by the Mott Iron Works, was highly stylized. Mayor Mitchell wanted it to be holding a light, as both a symbolic and practical measure. As it was, someone said the statue's headgear—an emblem on his forehead holding three art deco feathers—"is more consistent with a Flapper than an Indian." The chief was called Captain Pipe by the British. *Hopocan* means "pipe" in the Algonquin language. Recently, a group of historians and schoolkids tried to prove that Chief Hopocan and Chief Pipe were two separate people, yet his reputation as a singular person endures, although his son was also known as Captain Pipe. The chief's name was also used as a street name and, later, by the second of Barberton's famous chicken houses, Hopocan Gardens.

The Lenape and other tribes were defeated at the Battle of Fallen Timbers (in what is now Toledo) by General "Mad" Anthony Wayne. The Treaty of Greenville, following that defeat, opened the door to European settlers. The

The statue of Chief Hopocan greets visitors from the east at New Portage Park. *Photo courtesy of the author.*

first European to walk the portage path was French explorer René-Robert Cavelier, Sieur de La Salle, or Robert de La Salle. La Salle, in about 1666, explored the Great Lakes region, looking for the Ohio River. In 1669, he claimed the area for France.

Beginning around 1810, the settlers came to the Norton area. Settlers had arrived in Coventry Township somewhat earlier, about 1805. Among the first settlers were John and James Cahow and Abraham and Henry Van

Hyning. Henry became one of the region's first justices of the peace. The settlers came from New England, New York, the Netherlands, Germany and Ireland. Farms appeared as early as 1815. In 1816, Wolf Creek Township was established, which would develop into many towns, including Norton and, later, Barberton.

William Laird built a shipyard, a river freight business and a distillery in the northeastern part of the area after the War of 1812. The Palmer Glass Company became the first industry there. The most common businesses in any new settlement were shipyards, distilleries and glass factories. Glass was important—the residents needed something to put their whiskey in. Laird also called the village New Portage. Jacob Welch made pottery in New Portage and later served as postmaster.

The fate of the village was sealed when the Ohio and Erie Canal, which opened in 1827, made Laird's river-based operation redundant. The canal, also known as "Clinton's Folly" (after DeWitt Clinton), was the largest commercial thoroughfare in the northeast quarter of the United States. It brought commerce and industry to cities in New York, Pennsylvania and Ohio. It was one of the largest engineering efforts of its day. However, there were problems in the New Portage area. A waterborne disease, known to some as the "killer fog" or "black tongue fever," decimated the canal workers and the early residents of New Portage. Kymberli Hagberg's book *Wicked Akron* provides a description of the plague. New Portage, a newer version, was moved a bit down the Tuscarawas River, just as the Lenape had done years earlier.

The Edwards Hotel was built in New Portage sometime between 1850 and 1870. It was at the Edwards that an entrepreneur named O.C. Barber would meet with his confederates to plan the city of Barberton.

In 1882, Barber located his new Portage Strawboard Company (which would become American Strawboard) on the old Van Hyning farm in New Portage. Strawboard, heavy paper made from straw pulp, is used in making boxes. Barber would use strawboard to make boxes for his Diamond Matches.

Later, in 1888, Barber took an option on a large area of land, about 550 acres, from the city of Norton, including Laird's former settlement. He wanted the land to mine for natural gas. He did not find gas but found deposits of salt and other minerals. Barber then decided to mine for soda ash, sodium carbonate, from the limestone deposits. Soda ash was used in the manufacturing of glass. Glass was, as mentioned earlier, one of early America's largest industries. Later, soda ash would be used in water softeners and as a cleaning agent for taxidermists. Soda ash is related somehow to carbonic acid. Ohio Columbus Barber's mining operation was scrapped when he realized that other concerns could mine more efficiently using the Solvay Process, developed by the Belgian chemist Ernest Solvay and still in use today. Rather than give up his option on the land, Barber envisioned an expanded industrial city growing from the site.

In 1891, Barber, of whom more later, formed the Barberton Land and Improvement Company, which bore the sinister sobriquet "The Syndicate," to fulfill his vision of a model industrial city. Barber was joined in the Syndicate by his brother-in-law John K. "Jack" Robinson of Diamond Match, attorney Charles Baird and hardware merchant Albert T. Paige. Colonel George Tod Perkins, president of the B.F. Goodrich Company, a man who had been wounded at the brutal Battle of Chickamauga during the Civil War, was an associate of the group. Later, the Syndicate sold part interest to a Pittsburgh syndicate headed by Charleroi Plate Glass Company magnate George W. Crouse Sr. and M.J. Alexander. Alexander would become the general manager of the Barberton Syndicate.

Alexander was a "town boomer," an entrepreneur who promotes new towns and helps draw investment, labor and permanent residents. Town booming was quite the movement at the turn of the last century. Alexander's "Magic Formula" was to establish industries in a new town, which would draw workers, who would need housing and services. The workers would build churches, schools, shops and commerce. Driven by factory jobs, the town would boom.

Alexander had previously boomed Charleroi and Jeanette in Pennsylvania. Charleroi, named for King Charles of Belgium, was south of Pittsburgh on the Monongahela. It was the location of Charleroi Plate Glass, Crouse's company. Pittsburgh's sister city was Charleroi in Belgium, and there were Belgian workers in the Pennsylvania glass industry. The town of Charleroi paid tribute to the immigrants and the glass trade from both locales. Colonel Perkins of the Syndicate was one of the businessmen who supported Alexander when he was booming Charleroi.

Alexander had also boomed the town of Pullman in Illinois in 1880. Pullman, of course, was home to the Pullman Car Company, and the planned community designed by Alexander was on Chicago's South Side. George Pullman was a good friend and poker-playing partner of O.C. Barber.

Barberton would become the third planned community in the country. A planned community offered employment and better-than-average living conditions for the workers who moved to the area to work for the company.

Unlike the other communities, Barberton was not a sole company town; there were many factories, and workers had employment opportunities in several industries. In short, Alexander had a track record of creating industrial-centric cities. Not just the city manager, Alexander became an entrepreneur there as well. Alexander and Crouse invested in the Ceramic Insulator Company and the Pittsburgh Valve and Fittings Company, moving it to Barberton.

The Syndicate hired civil engineer William A. Johnston, with whom Alexander had worked in Pennsylvania, to design and plat the city. New Portage, as he found it in the winter of 1891, was a handful of buildings and a tavern, where he found lodgings. There were few homes at the time. The oldest residence in Barberton is the Maloney house, originally the Brotsman family's home. The house is now owned by White House Chicken, the third of the fried chicken houses. The Brotsmans were among the first residents of the city. As there were few residences in the area that is now downtown Barberton, the Brotsmans took in boarders, early factory workers. The Brotsman home was across the street from the National Sewer Pipe Company, which would build the National Hotel at the same time. Both businesses changed their names in 1903 to the American Sewer Pipe Company and the American Hotel, respectively. Business at National Sewer Pipe picked up after the United States took over construction of the Panama Canal. The government purchased tons of pipe from the company.

Johnston developed the business district and laid out the lots that would become homes in just a few years' time. He saw a downtown shopping district that led into a residential area, with factories on the outskirts, although there were a few factories in the downtown area already. Johnston wanted the centerpiece of the town to be the glacial lake, which he named Lake Anna in his plans. Anna was O.C. Barber's daughter. The lake had been called Way's Lake, formerly Ways-Davis Lake, and Davis Lake before that. Ezra Way and Christopher Columbus Davis were farmers and early residents in New Portage who owned the land on either side of the lake. Way had purchased 280 acres during the land boom that followed the War of 1812.

The land was situated between the Cuyahoga and Tuscarawas Rivers with access to Lake Erie and the Ohio River. Like the Lenape people before him, Barber saw the value of developing an area rich in water and minerals. The expansion of the Ohio Canal in the 1820s made transportation a major factor in the area's growth. New Portage looked poised and ready to fulfill Barber's vision. Resources from nearby mines and farms, plenty of water and ease of transportation were a formula

Barber thought could not fail. His vision included businesses, parks, farms, cultural institutions and industries, all radiating out from the lake. Johnston made Barber's dream a reality.

Johnston platted the city along the lines of Charleroi. There had been industry in New Portage already. By 1820, it was the third-largest industrial region in Ohio. The farms needed attendant services—grain mills, tanneries, wheelwrights. Barber and the Syndicate wanted to build an industrial powerhouse there, the biggest, most modern, most productive town in Summit County. The Syndicate started selling land and building factories by the end of 1891. The first workers lived in tents until boardinghouses and residences could be built.

Alexander and Johnson held a five-day land sale in the spring of 1891. Half of the lots available sold immediately, raising $165,000 for the new city. The Barberton Savings Bank had opened in 1891, before the town was built. By November, more than three hundred homes had been built (costing anywhere from $100 to $4,000). Most of the high-end houses were on or near Lake Anna. The city was incorporated in 1892. Before the incorporation, voting and other political activities were still held in Norton, the city that had leased the land to Barber. In a great move of political dirty trick-playing, Democrats hired all of the horses and wagons from the livery stable, preventing their Republican counterparts from attending a nominating meeting.

The new city, like the settlement that preceded it, was called New Portage. The name *Barberton* would be chosen by voters in 1893 to honor their city's visionary founder. By the way, Barber would later purchase the Sierra Lumber Company as a source for his matchsticks; the village around the factory, soon to be a part of the Diamond Match Company empire, was named Barber, California. It later became part of neighboring Chico. Barber also had a town named for him near Covington, Virginia, then the site of the O.C. Barber Fertilizer Company. Many cities paid homage to their visionary founder.

Barber saw the importance of the railroad to his planned city and, in 1890, built the Erie Depot. The Erie Railroad had tracks to Norton as early as the 1850s. Workers, travelers and manufactured goods now had a more modern mode of transportation. Many railroads operated throughout that part of Ohio—the Cleveland/Akron/Columbus line, the Baltimore & Ohio and the Pennsylvania Railroad. The city constructed the Belt Line, which connected all of the train lines in the area. By linking the Barberton line with the others, Barberton manufacturers could get goods out more efficiently.

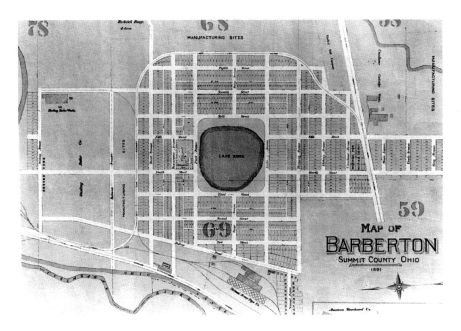

City map of the new planned community of Barberton, Ohio. *Photo courtesy of the Barberton Public Library.*

Barber's description was: "The sparkling lake, the undulating land and the forest-clad hills in the distance on every hand form a panorama of rare beauty....From the streets fronting the lake will extend evenly to the Belt Line." He said that the Belt Line "will exceed that of any manufacturing site in the country."

The history of early Barberton is the history of industries. From William Laird's freight company to the Diamond Match Company's move to the area in 1894, Barberton is at its core an industrial city. In quick order came the Kirkham Tile Company, American Alumina Company and Creedmoor Cartridge Company, in which Barber held controlling interest. They failed during the crash, although a devastating fire at Kirkham predated the panic. Joseph Kirkham, who founded the tile company, came from England and was a student of Josiah Wedgewood. The company, of which Barber was president, was the largest of its kind in the country. Creedmoor folded in 1892, although the Spanish-American War, which began five years later, and World War I would have reversed their fortunes.

At the turn of the last century, Barberton as a city was the largest soda ash producer, sewer pipe manufacturer, boiler maker, match maker and valve manufacturer in the United States. Rubber manufacturing spilled over from

Another major industry in Barberton was the Austin Insulator Lab, in 1950. Austin would purchase the Barber mansion from Anna Dean Bevan. *Photo courtesy of the Akron-Summit County Public Library.*

Akron. In the 1920s, Barberton was one of the largest industrial centers in the world.

Barber founded the Diamond Rubber Company, which would be acquired by the B.F. Goodrich Company. Brothers Frank and Chares Seiberling founded the Goodyear Rubber Company. When they lost control in 1921, they opened the Seiberling Rubber Company, formerly Portage Rubber, in Barberton.

There were successful companies in that first flush of Barberton development. The Stirling Water Tube Boiling Company would merge with Babcock and Wilcox, then located in Providence, Rhode Island, in 1906. Babcock and Wilcox, although no longer an industrial powerhouse in Barberton, is still a major employer there. B&W would be a major supplier of boilers for the navy in both world wars.

William Johnston brought the Columbia Chemical Company in 1899. It had been called the American Alkali Company and provided soda ash for the glass factories in the Pittsburgh area. It would become a division of Pittsburgh Plate Glass Industries in 1920. PPG would become one of the major employers in Barberton. It still has a research and development facility there.

From 1891 until the early 1900s, the population of Barberton grew so quickly that a reporter from the *Akron Beacon Journal* said that town had grown like magic. That is how it gained the nickname the "Magic City." The Syndicate, to lure residents to Barberton, placed newspaper ads that called it "The Garden Spot of the Western Reserve." The city founders had envisioned a population of no more than eight thousand. By 1894, the population had grown to exceed nine thousand.

John Szeman was the first Hungarian to settle in Barberton. He placed ads in newspapers urging other Hungarians to come to the "Magic City" for work. Szeman Americanized his name to Simon and was a successful saloonkeeper. He founded *Isten Alp Me a Magyar*, translated as "God Bless the Hungarian," an aid society for immigrants and one of the first in the area.

Things were not always a bed of cherry blossoms with Barberton industries. Here, members of the Boilermakers local go on strike against Babcock and Wilcox. *Photo courtesy of the Akron Beacon Journal.*

By 1930, a large percentage of immigrants from Eastern Europe had settled in Barberton. The book *A Bicentennial Remembrance of Barberton, Ohio* describes the influx of Eastern European immigrants: "They came from… cities with strange sounding names, like Kaposvar, Sarajevo, Tomaszow, or Bucharest." By 1932, 23 percent of the population was from other countries.

One of the immigrants' first acts, apart from building churches, was to establish cultural societies—the Slovenian National Benefit Society, the Hungarian Club in 1903, the Jednota Club (for Slovaks) and the Slovak Catholic Sokol Assembly in 1905. *Sokol* means "falcon" in Czech, and it was a physical fitness movement embraced by most of the cultures of Eastern Europe. The Serbian Home, perhaps the first of its kind in the United States, opened in 1911. The Serbian Home, *Serbsi Doma* in their native tongue, would be visited by Peter II, the last king of Yugoslavia. The earliest English-language lessons in town were given at the immigrant churches.

The nascent city faced its biggest challenge with the Panic of 1893. Dropping commodity prices led to a run on gold by investors. As conditions worsened, there were runs on banks. Companies—many in Barberton—failed, and the nation slid into a four-year depression. O.C. Barber came to the rescue of his city by relocating the Diamond Match

The Cherry Blossom Queen Pageant in 1987, one of the several civic celebrations that define Barberton. *Photo courtesy of the* Akron Beacon Journal.

The view down Tuscarawas Avenue in the 1930s, the main street of the city. *Photo courtesy of the* Akron Beacon Journal.

Company to Barberton from Akron. This was a vote of confidence and a needed infusion of money.

The Great Depression of the 1930s hit Barberton, but with its manufacturing jobs, it fared better than many other cities. World War II, as it had everywhere, brought jobs and high production to the city, and this prosperity lasted through the 1960s. The late 1970s saw a slowdown in the economy. The 1982 closing of the Sieberling Rubber Company was a major blow to the Barberton economy.

Barberton has always had a strong civic pride and a love of festivals. The Barberton Women's Club planted cherry trees around Lake Anna in the 1930s. Since then, they have held an annual Cherry Blossom Festival in the spring and an annual Mum Festival in the fall. Lake Anna became the cultural center of the city with its festivals, band concerts and, later, Chickenfest!—just as O.C. Barber and W.A. Johnson had planned.

Today, Barberton is on the rise again. Mayor William Judge says that people who left the city during those hard times are coming back. Local industries are getting government contracts, and small manufacturing, especially in technical fields, is on the rise. The city has a population of twenty-seven thousand, down from a high of forty thousand, but numbers have been holding steady for the past few decades. The downtown area now has a thriving arts district. Barberton lives up to the old motto of the Northwest Territory, "Meliorem lapsa locavi"—the city has planted one better than the one fallen.

PART 2: THE FOUNDER

My goods will be improved, which will give better satisfaction to the consumer, thereby increasing the value of my good will.
—*O.C. Barber, 1879*

Ohio Columbus Barber was born on April 20, 1841, in Middlebury, a small township that was later subsumed into the city of Akron. The neighborhood in East Akron is still referred to as Middlebury. Perhaps the name is a shout-out to Connecticut, from old Western Reserve days. Barber's parents, George and Eliza, had an interest in geography and in their adopted state, which explains their son's name. They were born in Connecticut and had moved to Akron in 1826.

George was a hotelkeeper who would manufacture matches in the barn at his farm starting about 1845. First working out of his farm workshop, he moved to a former woolen factory as his business grew. He made additional income by selling his matches door to door. O.C. Barber, called "Hi" by his family, became a sales representative for his father in 1857, traveling and selling throughout Ohio, Michigan and Indiana.

Strike matches, rather than sticks that were ignited by putting them into a fire, were first developed in the 1830s. They were manufactured by coating the head of a stick with wax and a mixture of chemicals, especially white phosphorus. The later safety match was created by coating a separate surface, the strike pad, with some of the chemicals used in the manufacture of the friction match. Commercial match production started in the United States in the mid-1830s. The man who held the patent, Alonzo D. Phillips, called his matches "loco foco crazies." *Loco foco* roughly translates as "self-fire," and it was also the tradename of a self-lighting cigar of the day. It is a shame that the name did not catch on, although a group of Democrats of the 1830s called themselves Loco-Focos.

By 1850, the number of match manufacturers skyrocketed to sixty companies. By the time of the Civil War, seventy-five separate companies, mostly in the East, were in the matchmaking business. After the war, and after some economic downturns, many closed. O.C. Barber, who had taken over his father's Barber Match Company, was a shrewd operator. He undercut his competitors' prices and looked for ways to streamline and modernize the process. Realizing that they were fighting each other, Barber and his archrival, William Swift, urged ten other rivals to merge. The new company, located in Akron, became known as the Diamond Match Company in 1868. Their match cartel dominated the market. Oddly, nearby Wadsworth's Ohio Match Company (manufacturers of the Blue Tip match), did not merge with Diamond; Diamond did buy the company in 1928. By the 1870s, Diamond Match was selling two million boxes of matches annually. Its president, O.C. Barber, became known as "America's Match King."

Ohio Columbus Barber, the "Match King" and the city's founder. *Photo courtesy of the* Akron Beacon Journal.

With the invention of the matchbook in 1894, which allowed portability and safety, Diamond took off as the leading match manufacturer in the world. The matchbook was invented in 1889 by a man named Joshua Pusey, a Philadelphia attorney, who was looking for a more portable way to light his cigars. He sold his patent to Barber in 1896 for $4,000.

The Diamond Match Company paid its employees less than other industrial concerns, but it offered far better benefits. It was the first company with a dental plan, a factory dining room and a hospital. As matchmaking involved the use of chemicals, workers were given milk breaks to combat sulfur poisoning. Phosphorous necrosis, commonly called "phossy jaw," was a hazard for match workers. Women and children worked at the factory at lower wages, but Barber would later change his mind about the employment of children.

Barber felt that a businessman needed to be involved in a minimum of five companies to keep his mind sharp. He was president of Akron Wool and Felt Company, American Alumina, American Strawboard, the Barberton Whiteware Company (whiteware was essentially dishes and pottery), Creedmoor Cartridge, Diamond Match, Diamond Rubber, the General

Fire Extinguisher Company, the Great Western Cereal Company, Kirkham Art Tile and Pottery Company, National Sewer Pipe and Stirling Boiler, among others. Great Western Cereal was founded to compete with the American Cereal Company, whose major product was Quaker Oats, still enjoyed today. For a time at the turn of the last century, Akron was the major cereal milling center of the country.

As a philanthropist, Barber founded Akron City Hospital. He served on Akron's city council after having served on the Middlebury Village Council. He was involved in the Akron Telephone Company. In short, O.C. Barber was an industry unto himself, always working, always seeing the future.

Barber married Laura Brown in October 1866. Their daughter Anna Laura was born the next year, followed by a son, Charles, who died in infancy. Barber was distraught that he had no son to carry on his family name. Laura died at the Plaza Hotel in New York in 1894 after a long recovery from abdominal surgery. She had not enjoyed good health for most of her life. She had been living at the Plaza since O.C. had moved the offices of Diamond Match to Chicago. Barber would marry again in 1915, to his former personal secretary, Mary Orr. Orr came from a family of businesspeople. She became his right-hand administrator.

In 1909, Barber devoted much of his time to overseeing the building of his fifty-two-room mansion. The extravagance of the place made the national news. Its house and landscaped grounds were the finest, as they said, between New York and Chicago. The marble used in the construction came from Sienna, Italy, from the same area that provided the marble for Michelangelo. The mansion, designed by the Akron architecture firm Harpster and Bliss, took more than a year to complete, at a cost of $400,000 (in 1910 terms). The mansion was demolished in 1965 after attempts to restore it by the Barberton Historical Society failed. Harpster and Bliss would also design Barberton's Masonic Temple.

Following the death of his brother-in-law and partner Jack Robinson, Barber stepped down from his enterprises. Barber's last project, unfortunately not a lasting one, was the Anna Dean Farm, an experiment in modern agricultural techniques. It was built at the same time, and in the same French Renaissance Revival style, as the mansion. Erected at a cost of $75 million, the farm comprised thirty-five independent structures on a 3,500-foot lot. Anna Laura Barber had married Arthur Dean Bevan in 1896. O.C. named his modern farm after the couple. Anna and Arthur had first been married in Chicago, but they held a second ceremony at the Barberton Inn, built on the lake named for Anna.

The Barberton Inn, on the banks of Lake Anna, built by Barber and later the site of Anna Barber Bevan's (second) wedding. *Photo courtesy of the Akron-Summit County Public Library.*

Barber had modeled his project after the Hartman farm near Columbus, Ohio, once the largest farm in the United States. Dr. Samuel B. Hartman used the farm to grow the ingredients for Peruna, the patent medicine that made him a wealthy man. Peruna was made up of alcohol (it was about 56 proof), water and herbs (especially *cubeb*, a type of pepper), with burnt sugar for coloring. Barber intended his property to be something more than a traditional farm. He wanted a center for modern, scientific agriculture.

The Brooder barn at Anna Dean could hold twenty thousand to fifty thousand chickens—free range, of course. The Piggery, one of the few building still standing, was later used to house Troop F of the Ohio National Guard. Barn No. 1 and the greenhouses were taken over by brothers Menno and Ira Yoder, who founded the Yoder Brothers Hot House Vegetable Company. Eventually, they switched to flowers and became world famous for growing chrysanthemums. The mum is the official flower of Barberton, the Japanese maple is the official tree. The Yoder concern is still in Barberton, now operating under the name Aris Horticulture, Inc.

Ohio Columbus Barber, visionary, industrialist, builder of cities, died of influenza in 1920 at the age of seventy-eight. Barber's biographer William Franklin Fleming states that Barber was "the last of Akron's remarkable

The gates and entryway to Barber's Anna Dean Farm (named after his daughter and son-in-law). It was the home of Barber's experimental modern farm. *Photo courtesy of the Akron-Summit County Public Library.*

The mansion before, 1951. *Photo courtesy of the* Akron Beacon Journal.

The mansion after. It was demolished in 1965. *Photo courtesy of the* Akron Beacon Journal.

nineteenth century entrepreneurs." The pallbearers at his funeral were a who's who of prominent men of the time, including the Seiberling brothers, Harvey S. Firestone, Barberton town planner W.A. Johnston and B.G. Work, the president of the B.F. Goodrich Company.

Barber worried that without an heir his dynasty would disappear. The mansion was eventually replaced by a housing development, and most of the Anna Dean Farm was sold off after Barber's death. Yet the town he created that bears his name and that served as a magnate for workers from all over the world is still there. It has been famed for its industry, for its culture and for its celebrated fried chicken, a mixture of Serbian techniques and American know-how.

Chapter Two

WHY ISN'T EASTERN EUROPEAN FOOD TRENDY?

There's no use in trying to convince anyone that Eastern European food is wildly popular or delicious. Because no one would believe you. It seems that…the further you get from the Atlantic Ocean, the less popular the country's cuisine.
—*Minyungee,* You Eatin' Nice *blog*

Eastern European cuisine, which encompasses foods from Germany to the outskirts of Asia, contains multitudes. Each country, each region within a country, has its own style of cooking, its own spin on traditional dishes. The best authority on the subject is Lesley Chamberlain and her book *The Food and Cooking of Eastern Europe*. Chamberlain points out that Eastern Europe covers "more than half the gastronomic globe." The influences range from Germany to the west, Russia from the east and Turkey and Greece from the south. Italian food has also exerted an influence, especially in the former Yugoslavia.

Eastern European food is not delicate. The cuisine is meat-heavy and involves starchy foods. Vegetarian dishes are not unknown, though. Vegetables—raw, pickled or cooked—play their part. Yet, most people think that Eastern European food is solely sausage, sauerkraut and potatoes. It is a cuisine rich in fat, cholesterol and salt—or so the story goes.

Yet, this may not be the case. The website Trip Savvy (www.tripsavvy.com) tells us that "Eastern European traditional foods are the best part of travel [to that region]." If people are encouraged to eat it there, why is it not eaten here as enthusiastically?

The five Barberton fried chicken houses served chicken cooked Serbian style following recipes brought from the former Yugoslavia. Over the past eighty years, Serbian chicken and signature side dishes have become American. The food may have been toned down for western tastes, but it is authentically Eastern European.

It's not that some Eastern European restaurants have not been popular. New York's Russian Tea Room, with its tsarist brothel decor, was one of the poshest restaurants in that city's golden age of dining. The restaurant was founded by members of the Russian Imperial Ballet in 1927. On the other hand, the Veselka Coffee Shop in the East Village has been serving traditional Ukrainian foods to New Yorkers since 1954. This shows the two contrasting views on Russian food: caviar and blini or kielbasa and pierogi—the foods of the ruling class and of those ruled.

Cleveland's Frank Sterle's Slovenian Country House, a short drive from Barberton, served everything from paprikash to schnitzel until its closing in 2017. Nearby, at tony Shaker Square, Balaton has won awards for its Hungarian cuisine. It was twice named *Food and Drink*'s Best International Restaurant and has been honored by *Gourmet* magazine. Washington, D.C.'s Ambar may be the only Michelin-rated Balkan restaurant in the United States. It serves *cevapcici* but anglicizes it to "sausage."

In most cities, you can find a place that serves traditional Eastern European foods. But Eastern European cuisine never became trendy. It's not cool, and it is, most definitely, not hip. It's not a destination restaurant. It is the food of our grandparents. Except, apparently, in Denver, where a food truck called Baba and Pops has been selling what it calls artisan pierogi.

The cuisines of Mexico, Thailand, Ethiopia, Japan, Latin America and, seemingly, the rest of the world, all have dedicated followers. In any major city, Italian and French food dominate the restaurant scene. Greek food seems to be having a revival at present, spurred on, no doubt, by the health benefits of the Mediterranean diet. Chinese food may be the most popular ethnic food of all. Cajun food, not the healthiest in the world, was all the rage for a time. Even German foods become trendy at Octoberfest. Germany may not be considered Eastern Europe, but much of the food has roots in the Austro-Hungarian Empire. There are classic German restaurants from the Jacob Wirth Co. in Boston to the Berghoff in Chicago (which started as a food stall at the 1893 World's Fair), to the Red Lion Tavern in Los Angeles. But where is the love for Eastern European food?

Perhaps Eastern Europe covers far too much ground. People who love the food of one area might not by necessity gravitate to the cuisine of another.

The Ottoman/Turkish influence on Serbian food may not appeal to those who love the seafood-dominated diet dictated by the Russian Orthodox Church. The original settlers in the area we now call Russia were Vikings from Sweden. They were Varangians, the Greek word for "Vikings." They were called the Rus ("the men who row"). They brought food from the northern reaches of Europe. Kiev, the capital of Ukraine, was on a major trade route between Constantinople and the land of the Norsemen. Spices, food items and styles of cooking were imported from the major nations of Europe and Central Asia. In short, there is a wide array of foods from Eastern Europe. Italian cooking is divided by direction (north or south), French cuisine by style (classic of country), but Eastern Europe is divided among sixty separate ethnic groups. Therefore, there is no one cuisine to rally around. However, as Chamberlain points out, "the differences in the finished food products are not as marked as the various ministries of tourism would like." In short, if you grow to like one Eastern European cuisine, chances are good that you will like another.

Another reason for the ostracization is that Eastern Europeans do not have a holiday that Americans celebrate with traditional foods. On St. Patrick's Day, everyone eats corned beef and cabbage. At Octoberfest, we eat sausage and drink beer. Every Jewish American knows that you eat Chinese food on Christmas Eve. Easter is when most cultures serve their traditional holiday dishes, but few here serve *cevapcici* with *ajvar* at Eastertime.

There is no easy answer to the lack of popularity of Eastern European food among the young and hip. Ghoulardi, a horror-film host in Cleveland in the 1960s, constantly poked fun at Parma, an Eastern European enclave on the city's south side. He was following the then-popular fad of Polish jokes. Ghoulardi would mention Parma, and polka music would start to play—the Frank Yankovic classic "Who Stole the Kishka?" Recently, though, the hipster hangout Melt Bar and Grilled, a grilled cheese sandwich chain, introduced the Parmageddon, a sandwich with pierogi and sauerkraut inside, as a tribute to that embattled city. In some circles, kielbasa has become a must-have item among the young, but if that is all that is known of Polish cooking, something has been lost.

Polish cuisine had its biggest hipster moment in 2007. Anthony Bourdain, host of the Travel Channel's *No Reservations*, ate at Sokolowski's University Inn with underground comic writer Harvey Pekar. Sokolowski's opened in 1923, serving Eastern European foods (stuffed cabbage, sausage, pierogi) to west-siders of all stripes. You cannot get cred any hipper that Bourdain and Pekar, and they enjoyed their cafeteria-style lunch. Sokolowski's serves *haluska*, but it Anglicizes it to cabbage and noodles. The James Beard Foundation honored the restaurant with an "America Classic" designation in 2014. Yet, the combined power of the award and the television program failed to put Sokolowski's on the culinary map, except for those who eat there regularly. The regulars already form a large crowd.

Eve Zibart, Muriel Stevens and Terrell Vermont published *The Unofficial Guide to Ethnic Cuisine & Dining in America* in 1995. They said: "But with the advent of Glasnost and the economic reconstruction of Eastern Europe, we can hope for a revival of not merely classic Russian and Polish dishes but Hungarian, Romanian, Czech, Azerbaijan, or even Ukrainian ones as well." We are still waiting for that revival.

Some cookbooks on Eastern European food have been well received. In 1965, Crown published *The Czechoslovak Cookbook* by Joza Brizova. Brizova's book, originally published as *Varime Zdrave Chutne a Hospodarne*, was the best-selling cookbook in the former Czechoslovakia, a sort of *Joy of Cooking* for Czechs. It has stayed in print in the States to this day. A few years back, Anya von Bremzen and John Welchman wrote the highly lauded *Please to the Table: The Russian Cookbook*. It won the 1991 James Beard Award for Best International Cookbook. Von Bremzen followed it up with *Mastering the Art of Soviet Cooking*. Yet, has anyone seen an upswing in Russian restaurants? If you consider the cuisine of Germany part of Eastern Europe, you have to consider that Mimi Sheraton's *The German Cookbook* has remained in print since 1965. Germany, as stated above, is really Middle Europe, looking toward the East.

Maura Judkis, the James Beard Award–winning *Washington Post* writer, published an article on the decline of German restaurants, "Worst Comes to Wurst." She points out that German cuisine, like the other Eastern European cuisines, does not have a star chef to inspire others to follow the trend. Wolfgang Puck is probably the best-known Austrian chef in the States, and what is he known for? Pizza. Judkis cites the case of Milwaukee chef and James Beard Award semifinalist Thomas Hauck, who bought the century-old German restaurant Ratzsch's. Hauck saw how old-fashioned and kitschy the place looked. To quote Judkis: "He was convinced that if he could just clean the place up and freshen up the menu, he could bring in a new crowd. The new, young crowd never arrived and the old crowd felt betrayed by the changes. Ratzsch's closed, and it was followed by the demise of Hauck's flagship restaurant c. 1800."

Yugoslavia existed as a country for less than one hundred years. It was formed, a confederation of states, in 1918, following World War I. It existed until 2006, when Serbia declared its independence. The country had been fragmenting since the 1990s, and many of the states were warring with one another. Each separate Yugoslavian state had a cuisine that was mostly imported from elsewhere. Part of Serbia was inspired by the foods of Turkey, while other parts were more Hungarian or Austrian. Chamberlain says that Serbia offered the best fish cookery of any Eastern European nation. She quotes travel writer and translator Lovett F. Edwards, who said that Belgrade was "a city of gourmets."

Whether the cuisine of Belgrade Gardens, or the other chicken houses, is gourmet fare remains to be seen. But Eastern European cuisine established itself in Barberton and the Akron area, with traditional Hungarian foods and Barberton's specialty, Serbian fried chicken.

The Barberton fried chicken houses have been serving their special food for decades. Alongside the fried chicken, they sell paprikash, dumplings, *cevapi* sausage and stuffed cabbage. Most of the diners at the restaurants are older. Those ethnic foods seem like the cuisine of the forebears, those who still remember. The restaurants are losing the twenty-five- to thirty-five-year-old segment of the market. There are many reasons for that (one being the perceived unhealthiness of the food), but the young also eat other cuisines that are old-world, fattening, peasant fare. How can we bring them back to the joys of Barberton fried chicken?

The Eastern European influence can be found throughout Northeastern Ohio. Eastern European restaurants can be found across America, yet it remains one of the least loved European cuisines.

Chapter Three

THE EASTERN EUROPEAN INFLUENCE
ON THE CUISINE OF BARBERTON

The colorful fare of…Eastern Europe, originally confined to big-city immigrant
enclaves, began to "go national" during the early decades of [the twentieth]
century, then after World War II, reached "Our Towns" across the country.
—*Jean Anderson,* The American Century Cookbook

When immigrants come to the States, the first flag they plant in their new country is their native food. They eat what is familiar, for practical as well as nostalgic reasons. As was the case with the Serbian immigrants who brought their traditional foods with them and created Barberton fried chicken, Eastern European immigrants who wanted a taste of home opened restaurants that offered their native cuisines. In Barberton, the Hungarian and German presence is felt most strongly, along with a few hybrids. Angie's, one of the best Italian restaurants in Barberton, which is owned by an Irish family, is a fine example of a hybrid.

Then as now, the immigrants who settle in a new community work hard to establish themselves. They open businesses to serve their fellow immigrants and the community at large. In years past, new immigrants drawn to the Magic City for work opened stores and businesses that reflected their cultures. Momchilov's Meat Market, founded by Tosa Momchilov in 1905, was considered the headquarters for Slovenian sausage. The small store on South Second Street had its own smokehouse. Tosa's son Eli, the "Sausage King," took over the business in 1942. He and his wife, Frances, using their secret recipe, made and sold their sausage for more than forty years. They sent special orders for their Slovenian sausage all over the country (both coasts), Japan and Germany. Like Belgrade Gardens, they had even sent food to our soldiers in Vietnam.

Lena and Ben Recht from Poland opened Recht Grocery in 1915. Joseph J. Zupic opened a drugstore, and Milos Sekiki opened the Servian Baking Company. Peter Obradovich opened a Lawson's dairy store in 1947, which later became the Milk Jug. Lawson's, by the way, was a chain of dairy and deli stores based in Cuyahoga Falls, a northern suburb of Akron. Lawson's was known throughout Northeastern Ohio, as common as 7/11 stores are today. When the Magic City Shopping Center opened in 1951, one of its initial stores was a Lawson's. The American stores are all closed now, but the chain still exists in Japan, with its offices in Tokyo. Oddly, in a Japanese monster movie, Godzilla attacks a store with the familiar Lawson's milk jug sign, easily recognizable to every Northeast Ohioan.

The strongest bastion of Hungarian food is the Al's empire. Albert V. Pramuka opened Al's Quality Market as well as the now-closed Krinkle Doughnuts and the Coventry Drive-In. He had previously been the manager of the meat section at Acme No. 9, which had been located on Tuscarawas Avenue in the Tracy Block. The building was called the Tracy Block, built by Benjamin Franklin Tracy of the American Strawboard Company. The building housed offices, businesses and a performance hall, and it was the site of the first jail in Barberton.

Acme Supermarkets, not to be confused with the chain of stores of that name run by Albertson's Inc., is the still-thriving local grocery chain that dominates the grocery market in the Akron/Summit County area. The Acme stores were founded in 1891 by Frederick Wilhelm Albrecht of Massillon, Ohio. Albertson's Acme was the inspiration for Albrecht. He saw one of their stores in Philadelphia and changed the name of his eponymous store. The name fit Albrecht's market better: Akron, from the Greek *Acros*, meaning "High Point,' located in Summit County, would be an ideal place for Acme, which means "zenith." By the way, when Sinclair Lewis set his novel *Babbitt* in the fictional city of Zenith, Ohio, most Akron residents assumed he was talking about them.

In those days, the Albrecht Acme stores were primarily greengrocers. They leased the meat departments to butchers. Al, who was of Slovakian descent, returned from World War II and, in 1948, leased the meat department of the Acme store in Barberton. The Magic City Shopping Center opened in 1951 on the site of the former National Sewer Pipe Company. When Acme moved its store into the center, Al opened his own

IGA grocery store. IGA (Independent Grocers Alliance) was founded in 1923 to give small stores, in rural communities mostly, a marketing organization like those of the big chains. Al and partners Bob and Dick Buerhle, Al's brother-in-law, eventually created Al's Quality Market.

Al's Quality Market specializes in meat, with Al's Hungarian and Slovenian sausage being the centerpiece. The butcher's case is filled with steaks, roasts and other meats, but the sausage is the strongest draw for people from the region. They also have City Chicken, a dish known to people in the Midwest but that may not be familiar to the rest of the nation. City Chicken is not chicken at all. In the 1920s and '30s, when chicken was expensive but veal was not, people skewered chunks of pork and veal, breaded it and fried it like chicken. The dish is still popular in Ohio, although prices of chicken and veal have been reversed. Many grocery stores in Northeast Ohio offer premade City Chicken.

Al's Quality Market sells Eastern European beer and wines and some other grocery items, European or not. Recently, Al's put up a display of ersatz vintage beers—older local brands like Cincinnati's Little Kings Cream Ale, Stroh's (the Bohemian beer from Detroit), Carling Black Label (which had sponsored the Cleveland Indians for years) and Blatz, that most onomatopoeic of all beers. It appears that these beers are from a contract brewery in Wisconsin and may not follow the original recipes. A puzzled employee said that the nostalgic beers had been selling better than the imports.

Al's Corner Restaurant was located at Fourth Street and Tuscarawas Avenue. It was opened by Tim and Jeanette Eberhardt, who had purchased the business from Al in 2001. It is now at 155 Second Street, next to Al's Quality Market (151 Second Street). The window sign proudly proclaims that it is the "Corner Restaurant (in the Middle of the Block)." On weekdays, lunch at Al's is cafeteria-style, with many of the traditional Hungarian foods (and a generous sampler plate) on offer. Food blogger Tom Noe calls Al's the "Hungarian Nirvana." The sampler plate comprises chicken paprikash (until it sells out), Hungarian sausage, stuffed cabbage, pierogi with onions and sauerkraut and *haluska*, the sweet and savory mixture of cabbage and noodles (and sometimes raisins). It provides one hearty meal or several rounds of leftovers. A large map of the Balkans on the back wall of the sparsely decorated dining room offers a visual lesson in topography and history.

A note about paprikash—spelled in Hungarian, probably in Serbian as well, as paprikas: paprikash is chicken that has been stewed in chicken

The Hungarian lunch selection at Al's Corner Restaurant. *Photo courtesy of the author.*

stock, peppers, onions, tomatoes and, as the name implies, paprika. In the authentic recipe, the chicken is first sautéed in lard. The dish is a Hungarian classic and may be their national dish. The Serbians make their own version. The paprikash served at Belgrade Gardens is in a thin, spicy broth. The Hungarians thicken their paprikash with sour cream and flour. Both cultures serve their versions with dumplings.

The Al's empire is now owned by Denny Gray, who calls himself the "Al's Historian." He is joined by his wife, Beth, and, on occasion, his son. A former salesman who bought the businesses from the Eberhardts, Gray thinks that Barberton should be known for its sausage and not for fried chicken. Eli Momchilov was known as the "Sausage King," but Gray has taken up the mantle, making sixteen types of sausage and more. His Hungarian sausage has been mentioned lovingly by Katie Byard in the *Akron Beacon Journal*, by Jane and Michael Stern in their guidebook *Roadfood* and in *Saveur* magazine.

Gray says that in Barberton's not too distant past, there were five or six stores within walking distance of Al's where shoppers could get traditional Hungarian or Slovenian sausage. Now, only he remains.

The new restaurant kid on the block is the Green Diamond Grille (125 Second Street, Barberton, Ohio, 44203), which opened in 2004. One of Akron's best-known restaurants is the Diamond Grille, a world-famous steakhouse, the place where Sinatra ate when he performed at the Richfield Coliseum north of Akron. The Green Diamond Grille in Barberton is not in any way related to the steakhouse. But it is a source of local culinary pride. Owner John Kriston (born Janos Klistom) had worked with the Ted Williams Foundation and was executive director of the Ted Williams Museum in Hernando, Florida. Williams was the legendary left fielder for the Boston Red Sox. The Green Diamond is named for the baseball diamond, with perhaps Boston's Fenway Park in mind.

The restaurant and its much-heralded pub next door are decorated in two frames of mind. There are portraits of sports figures, most notably Teddy Baseball, Barberton's own Jeep Davis and Bo Schembechler. Davis and Schembechler are folk heroes in Barberton, although both ended up involved in football in Michigan. Glenn "Jeep" Davis moved to Barberton at fifteen, following the deaths of his parents. He would go on to win three gold medals at the Olympics from 1956 to 1960, two for hurdles and one for the relay. Jeep later became a wide receiver for the Detroit Lions. A statue of Davis stands in front of the Barberton Public Library. Native Barbertonian Glenn "Bo" Schembechler was coached by legendary Ohioan Woody Hayes at Miami University. After serving as Hayes's assistant coach at Ohio State, Schembechler became coach of OSU's nemesis, the University of Michigan.

Pictures and references to Schembechler are everywhere in town. Schembechler, Davis and Fenway Park signs and pictures dominate the Green Diamond's dining room. However, sports imagery mixes somewhat uncomfortably with paintings of goddesses from Greek and Middle Eastern mythology. Ishtar, the Mesopotamian goddess of war and sexual love, brandishes a scimitar, a tambourine and a provocative smile on a mural in the main dining room. She seems to be wearing a brassiere made of seashells, with two contented lionesses resting at her feet. In another mural, three muse-like goddesses, one nude and petting a leopard, gaze at the diners. In the past, all the goddesses had been nude, but when some of the family patrons complained, the muralist was called back to drape the offending au naturel maidens.

The food at the Green Diamond Grille is what one would expect in a downtown restaurant—steaks, chops, Lake Erie perch and walleye. However, the restaurant has a unique special on Wednesday—"Hunky Night" at the Green Diamond. Paying tribute to Kriston's Hungarian roots, the menu offers paprikash, cabbage rolls, Hunky chicken and dumplings and spicy sausage from Al's Quality Meats, served with *haluska*. A combination platter comprises whatever is available. The supply is limited, just like at Al's. When the demand is high, it is not unusual for the Green Diamond to run out of items, particularly the paprikash. Should the diner have room for dessert, the Hungarian crepes—*palascintas*—filled with strawberry jam complete the traditional experience. For the past few years, the Green Diamond Grille has won countless awards from both the *Akron Beacon Journal* and the *Barberton Herald*.

A local institution is Fa-Ray's, a family-style restaurant offering standard diner fare. It has been a gathering spot in Barberton since 1949. The restaurant's name is pronounced "Fay Wray," as in the star of *King Kong*. It is in fact named for the founders' children, Fred and Ray. Although the owners were Slavic, the restaurant offers few ethnic foods. They do have a version of hot rice on the menu. There are more Italian foods than Slavic. The menu offers broasted, not Barberton, chicken, which has its admirers.

In 1967, a Czech immigrant named Vera Chuti opened the Old Prague Restaurant in Vermillion, Ohio, about fifty miles northwest of Barberton. Is serves old-world foods in the traditional fashion, such as the traditional winter dish *svickova na Smetana*, beef and vegetables baked and sauced and served with *houskové knedlíky* (bread dumplings). The Old Prague calls itself "The Original Czech Restaurant." One of the appetizers served at the Old Prague is sauerkraut balls, a dish that is as customary on Northeastern Ohio tables as Serbian fried chicken.

A sauerkraut ball is a fritter of sorts, made of ham or sausage, garlic, onions and sauerkraut. Breaded and fried, they are served with a sauce, generally mustard. Although it seems like a German dish (and some think Polish), Akron claims to have invented the appetizer. In an interview with WKSU-FM's Mark Urycki, sauerkraut ball maker Keith Kropp said that "sauerkraut balls are to Akron like Buffalo wings are to Buffalo and Philly [steak] sandwiches are to Philly." The company Kropp runs, Or Derv Foods, had been Bunny B, which distributed bags of ice as well as sauerkraut balls. J.T. Salem, who owned Bunny B, was not Eastern European, by the way; he was Lebanese. His brother K.T. (Kareem Tanous) founded Akron's Salem Potato Chip Company. Even Angie's, Barberton's venerable Italian restaurant, serves sauerkraut balls as an appetizer.

Three restaurants in nearby Akron are worth noting. The Bavarian House, near the Goodyear plant on East Market Street, closed in 1994. The neighborhood had fallen on hard economic times. The rubber companies were cutting back, and heavy infrastructure projects hampered traffic. The *Akron Beacon Journal*'s Jane Scott said that "road construction did what cholesterol could not do." Vera Zieham had opened the restaurant, which resembled a country inn and which had served traditional German dishes and beers. Wiener schnitzel, jager schnitzel and spaetzli kept rubber workers—and other fans of hearty European fare—well fed for years.

The now defunct Mijo's House of Paprikash was situated on the corner of South Main and West Exchange Streets in Akron, within walking distance of the B.F. Goodrich Company. Hart Crane's poem "Prophyro in Akron" starts with the line: "Greeting the dawn / A shift of rubber worker presses down / South Main." A reader could believe they were heading to Mijo's. Hans Conried, an actor of Austrian descent, was performing in a play at the Akron Civic Theatre. He ate at Mijo's and loved it so much he returned the next day.

The third, and most noteworthy, Akron restaurant is the New Era, the best-known paprikash house in the area. (The assumption is that Belgrade Gardens is predominately a fried chicken house with a paprikash option.) The New Era—10 Massillon Road, off East Market, under an I-76 overpass and in the shadow of the Goodyear Rubber Company—is now owned by Mary Lekic, who bought the place with her husband, Mitch. Founded by Lucille Juric in 1938, at the end of the Depression, when a New Era offered hope and prosperity, the restaurant offered dishes cooked from family recipes brought from the Dalmatian Coast of Croatia. The food was traditional: the Serbian paprikash, always served with apple strudel for dessert, city chicken, *cevapi* (pronounced "chev-AP-ee"), pork and lamb sausages with onions. The place leaned toward art deco in decor but was also decorated with Yugoslavian travel posters. Connie Bloom in the *Akron Beacon Journal* said, "One step inside [the New Era] and you're sure you're in the wrong time period." The strudel was made in-house, but the pies were imported from Barberton. Once, baker Liz Strebeck had a broken arm and could not make the strudel. It was one of the rare instances of a New Era tradition being broken.

The New Era closed in 2005, and the building was torn down. Long-term employee Christine Rexrode said in the *Akron Beacon Journal* that she watched the destruction of the old building with tears in her eyes. The original New Era employed fourteen people, with Mary Lekic doing most of the cooking.

The New Era was remodeled and resurrected with twenty employees and the same tradition. A respondent, Cindy K., on Trip Advisor, said of the New Era's paprikash, "If I was on death row and had to pick, my last meal that's what I'd order." Jessica Coomes, a writer for the *Akron Beacon Journal*, summed up the appeal of the restaurant: "[New Era is] a place for working men to have a hearty meal at a reasonable price."

That description fits also the Eastern European restaurants of Barberton, especially the homes of Serbian fried chicken. When one thinks of the cuisine of the United States, one thinks of a literal melting pot, of stews. Most stew, that form of preparing meats and vegetables, is peasant food adapted to a workingman's palate and price range. Add to that Serbian fried chicken and you have an original approach to Ohio food.

Each part of the country has its regional international food—Latin American food in Florida, the Scandinavian influence in the Plains States and the Asian impact on the foods of Hawaii and the West Coast. Eastern Europeans were scattered throughout Northeastern Ohio, Akron, Barberton and Cleveland. Pete Franklin, the argumentative/abusive sports talk star of Cleveland radio, always referred to Cincinnati as "That Little German Sausage Town on the Ohio River." He meant it in a derogatory fashion, but Cincinnati craft sausage remains.

In Northeast Ohio, the cuisine of Eastern Europe has a prominent place. Barberton may not be the only center, but it is a vibrant one. The slogan at the Old Prague Restaurant is *Dobrou Chut'*, Czech for "bon appetit." There is a line in the movie *The Natural* in which a coach says about spaghetti: "You can't spell it, but it eats pretty good." That's a good description of the Eastern European cuisine of Northeastern Ohio. Barberton fried chicken does not have a foreign-sounding name, and it appears to be an all-American dish. It is, though, a special meeting, Eastern European and working-class Ohio, at a culinary crossroad.

Chapter Four

BARBERTON FRIED CHICKEN

It's fun trying to explain "our" chicken culture to people from other places.
—Linda Halle, "Akron, Ohio Memories" Facebook page

T he most frequently asked question is, what makes Barberton fried chicken different? The truthful answer is, not much, apart from its excellence. Barberton fried chicken is simple, breaded chicken fried in lard. The process involves fresh chicken dipped in flour, then the floured pieces are run through an egg wash and then dipped in bread crumbs. The breaded chicken pieces are chilled. The refrigeration process helps the coat adhere to the chicken; it also has the same result as brining. Deep frying then forms a seal for the juices. The specialness—the magic—of the chicken can be experienced but not explained. It is expertly fried chicken with a crisp crust and juicy meat. The secret spice involved is salt; no other mixture of herbs and spices is necessary to improve the flavor of the fresh chicken. Barberton fried chicken is special because of the technique more than because of the recipe.

Sue Gorisek wrote in *Ohio Magazine*, "There is no such thing as Barberton's best because all Barberton chicken is exactly alike." This is not entirely accurate, and even Gorisek admits that there are personal chicken affinities. Family members have favorite chicken houses. "Divided family loyalties fuel family feuds, forcing strict dining out schedules so that different tastes can be satisfied."

Jane Snow, the *Beacon Journal* food writer, pointed out that restaurants "have all the charm of a roadside Howard Johnson." That is a harsh judgement, but you go to a Barberton fried chicken house for the food, not for the atmosphere (although each does have its unique physical charm).

As Barberton is an industrial city, Kenneth Nichols in his Town Crier column in the *Akron Beacon Journal* said, "The [Barberton] chicken dinner is an industrial product, even if for devotees it adds a tantalizing perfume instead of smoke to the air."

The major difference between Barberton's Serbian-style fried chicken and anyone else's can be found in the side dishes. To call Barberton's version coleslaw is to do it an injustice. Coleslaw comes from the Dutch word *koosla* ("cabbage salad"). Many people mistakenly use the term *cold slaw*, as it is generally a chilled dish. In Barberton, the slaw is derived from the Serbian *Kupus salata* ("cabbage salad"). Yes, both are cabbage salads, but the blending of oil, vinegar, sugar and cabbage served at the chicken houses is an elevated form of the dish. Only Belgrade Gardens adds carrots to the slaw. The restaurants follow their own recipes and cut their cabbage in individual ways. The primary taste is of vinegar, but if done properly, the sugar will cut the astringency. The cabbage, although marinated, is still crisp, green and refreshing. It is a palate cleanser of the first rank.

Many restaurants in other regions serve slaw with their fried chicken dinners. Few serve hot sauce. That is the special Serbian-based hot sauce of Barberton. *Djuvec* (pronounced "Joo-veech") is a traditional Serbian dish with its roots in Turkish *Guvec*. The Turks, specifically of the Ottoman Empire, had occupied the former Yugoslavia for one hundred years, from the late sixteenth to the end of the seventeenth centuries. They left a heavy influence on the Balkans, most notably on the foods of the region. *Djuvec* is a Balkan rice dish, but it can also include meat and become a main dish, a casserole. The Bulgarians call the dish *gyuvetch*. Elsewhere, it is *ghiveci*. The basic ingredients are rice, peppers, onions and tomatoes. In Bosnia and Croatia, it is a common side dish. In Barberton, *djuvec*, called hot sauce, is the ideal accompaniment for fried chicken. Food writer Diane Unger, in her "On the Side" column, compares Barberton hot sauce to Hungarian *sataras*, which has no rice. Like many Eastern European dishes, *sataras* crossed borders. Unger was not a fan of Barberton hot sauce. She thought it had too little rice, was too thin and was too much like gruel. She may have been wrong.

Hot sauce can be eaten as a side dish or as a dipping sauce for chicken and French fries. It is similar in taste to *ajvar*, the Serbian eggplant and pepper spread. Many diners compare hot sauce to Spanish rice (which is actually a Mexican, not a Spanish, dish—*aroz rojo*, "red rice"). The hot sauce varies from chicken house to chicken house—Village Inn Chicken's is thicker than the rather soupy hot sauce at White House Chicken. More than any other aspect of their cuisine, the owners of the chicken houses guard the secrets of their hot sauce recipe assiduously.

Jane Snow, the long-serving food writer for the *Akron Beacon Journal*, once wrote a famous article entitled "I Cracked the Case: When the Chickens Weren't Taking and the Stool Pigeon Couldn't Be Bought." In the article, she published basic versions of Barberton chicken house recipes, including that well-guarded hot sauce recipe. She also wrote of Barberton's "Deep Fried Secret." However, knowing the recipes and being able to approximate the food is no substitute for the real Barberton chicken house dinner.

In years past, the French fries may have been cooked in lard as well. Now, vegetable oils are being used, mostly canola oil. The fries are thin and crispy, with bits of skin still attached to the never-frozen potato. They are served hot, sometimes too hot to touch, and the taste of the fries is of good, solid, natural potato—no spices, no herbs. There are those who put ketchup on French fries; at the chicken houses, most people dip their fries in the hot sauce or sometimes in applesauce, if one's palate is sensitive to the heat. The combination of starch, spice and peppery tang of the dipped fries is at the heart of the Barberton fried chicken experience.

The star of the show is the fried chicken. Barberton is known as "The Fried Chicken Capital of the World." Other cities and towns make that claim—Frankenmuth, Michigan, for one. Barberton, though, has been the focus of much media attention. The Food Channel's program *Food Feuds* held a competition between Belgrade Gardens and the White House; Belgrade won. Celebrated food writer John T. Edge, director of the Southern Foodways Alliance, wrote about Barberton fried chicken twice, once in the essay "The Barberton Birds" in US Airways' *Attaché Magazine*, and again in his book *Fried Chicken: An American Story*. (The book's entry was an adapted version of the magazine piece.) Edge said about fried chicken in general, "I have concluded that [good fried chicken outside of the South was] nothing more than satisfying aberrations, mistakes of culinary geography…cases of novelty trumping reality." Edge changed his tune and came to appreciate the mastery of Barberton chicken.

One characteristic of Barberton fried chicken is the quality of the bird itself. Many would claim that, despite its meager reputation, it can be a dinner worthy of a food lover's attention. Edge put it best: "All Barberton Chicken tastes absurdly simple, almost ascetic." One could not say that this represents the Zen of fried chicken, but sometimes, the simplest of foods speak the loudest. Food lovers pay attention to dinners that are organically raised, free-range, locally sourced and GMO free. Barberton fried chicken passes all of those tests.

When one thinks of larger, chain fried chicken operations, one does not want to know about the origins and processing of the commercial birds. By contrast, the smaller Barberton chicken houses get their chickens from local Amish-owned farms. A major supplier is Gerber Amish Farms, a company that has been selling chicken, both retail and wholesale, since 1952. Dwight and Melba Gerber had a farm. They processed their own chickens and sold them door-to-door to their neighbors. The company grew and now contracts with more than 150 individual small farms, mostly Amish- or Mennonite-owned, to raise chickens to their exacting standards. They do not claim that Gerber chickens are organic, but the birds are fed a specially designed, all-vegetable feed and are given no hormones or antibiotics. The owners do not claim that Gerber chickens are free-range, but their website stresses that the chickens are free to roam indoors and out to their hearts' content. They are raised in roomy chicken houses, with plenty of air and abundant light. The owners do not claim that the birds are locally sourced, but Gerber's Amish Farm in Kidron, Ohio, is a scant twenty-five miles from Barberton.

Gerber chickens are raised and processed humanely. Yes, processing means killing, but some methods are more humane than others. FACTA (Farm Animal Care Training and Auditing group) monitors the farms to ensure that the chickens are raised in a safe and healthy environment. The deceased chickens are bathed in a cold-water citric and acetic acid bath, both natural, and are packaged hygienically. The chickens served at the Barberton restaurants are what one would expect from a gourmet store like Whole Foods or from a more fashionable dining spot. This explains why the cost of a Barberton chicken has gone up over the years. You pay for that quality.

There is one other difference of note between Barberton fried chicken and other restaurants' offerings. The Barberton restaurants serve the chicken back as a separate piece. The back is not the meatiest part of the chicken, and most restaurants, including White House Chicken, cut the bird in such a way that the back becomes part of the breast. In many restaurants, the back and the ribs are discarded. However, when Belgrade Gardens first opened, chickens were expensive; it was considered a rare treat to have a chicken for dinner. This was the Great Depression, and cooks had to get the maximum use from the food they cooked. Emelyn Rude published a fascinating history of chickens as food, *Tastes Like Chicken: A History of America's Favorite Bird*. Rude describes the oysters, those small rounds of meat along a chicken's backbone: "[They] accumulate all of the essential oils and flavors of a chicken's rich life. The French call them '*sot-l'y-laisse*,' which translates to 'the fool leaves them there.'" The food writers John T. Edge and the Sterns also sang the praises of the Barberton fried chicken back. In his book *Fried Chicken*, Edge called the backs "chicken ribs." He became a fan. "Though they yield little meat, they offer a wealth of crust to be chomped from the bone."

The most respected experts on casual dining are the peripatetic Jane and Michael Stern. They have written about Barberton fried chicken many times. In their classic reference directory *Roadfood*, the Sterns describe the beauty of Barberton chicken: "[It's] fried chicken that is drippingly juicy with a dense red-gold crust that crunches and melts into pure savory flavor." Elsewhere, they praise the use of shortening. "The frying medium is lard, insinuating every bite with wanton luxe." Billy Joe Mikoda, the chef/owner of the popular Valley Café in Akron, is a transplanted southerner of Polish extraction, and he likes that they use lard. It is the best way to get that crispy coating, he believes. The hosts of the Food Network's *Two Fat Ladies* said the same thing about the importance of lard in frying foods.

A note about lard. Most people think that it is unhealthy, synonymous with clogged arteries. Jennifer McLagan wrote a book called *Fat: An Appreciation of a Misunderstood Ingredient*, an argument in favor of oils and shortening. McLagen points out that lard is good for us. Its combination of fatty acids promotes the good cholesterol and has antimicrobial properties. Lard is natural, which means it has no trans fats. Foods fried in lard, she tells us, absorb less fat than if fried in other oils. Lard has become something of a gourmet item of late. Bill Buford's *New Yorker* profile of chef Mario Batali mentions that the chef arrived at a party with his homemade *lardo*, which Buford describes as the "raw 'lardy' back of a very fat pig."

A quote in an article by the *Beacon Journal*'s David Giffels almost serves as a metaphor for the city itself, its resilience in the face of changing circumstances: "The breading of the chicken is the armor. The Deep-frying is the baptism by fire."

The Barberton chicken houses were serving about thirty thousand customers a week, approximately seven tons of chicken per week. Business at the chicken houses has fluctuated, and economic downturns had their effect on the restaurants. They still have their loyal followers. One woman, Donna Daggett Logan, praised her first Barberton fried chicken experience: "I never liked fried chicken until my very first serious boyfriend took me [to

Barberton] and [I] fell in love with the food. The boyfriend is gone but my love for chicken remains!'

Other diners, still in Barberton or part of the diaspora, hold memories of the chicken houses. On Facebook's "Akron, Ohio Memories" page, Donna Jones Siebert said: "Once a month my mom & dad would take the family to Barberton for a chicken dinner. We would rotate. One-month Belgrade's, the next Hopocan then Terrace then White House." Renie Post commented on the same page that, although she loves the South: "I can't find a decent restaurant that serves fried chicken....Man, I miss Belgrade [Gardens]." That speaks volumes about southern dominance in the fried chicken world.

There were competitors who were known for their fried chicken. There was a restaurant in Canton called Chicken Manor, which opened in 1953 and closed in 2015. There was also Kern's Canton Chicken. Ron Kern, the proprietor, worked at White House Chicken. He was the son of Velma Pavkov Kern, grandson of the owners. He would later manage Milich's Village Inn.

The Orchard Tavern opened in nearby Kenmore in 1937, just four years after Belgrade Gardens. The streetcar could take residents from Barberton to Kenmore, where dollar chicken dinners were a big draw. The site of the Orchard Tavern is now Innes Middle School on East Avenue, just a few blocks from the Barberton line. Recently, Matt Margolis, owner of the upscale women's store Charlotte's West, and Joseph Berish tried to replicate the Barberton experience in Akron. His restaurant, Coop-De-Doo, failed. Apart from having a silly name, the restaurant found that the Barberton experience does not export well.

A writer named Gregory Pappas wrote a book called *The Magic City*, a study of the impact of the closing of the Sieberling Rubber Plant in Barberton. In the book, Pappas states, "There are no truly ethnic restaurants or shops in Barberton." The chicken houses are family restaurants, as Pappas saw it, that were most frequently patronized after church on Sunday. He passed on this judgement: "Outsiders discourteously refer to them as 'redneck restaurants.'" Pappas must not have gone to the five chicken houses, all of which wore their Eastern European cultures with pride, both in cuisine and in decoration. He states that the Italians were the largest immigrant group to settle in Barberton. The Slovenes and Slovaks were the second and third largest, respectively, but added together, they dominated the culture. It was not until the post–World War II era that the white southerners, or "rednecks," as some people call them, migrated heavily to the area.

Belgrade Gardens may not be what Pappas considers an ethnic restaurant, but current owner Milos Papich proudly serves the same recipes his grandmother brought from her home in Serbia. In fact, the biggest Americanization of the Serbian recipe is the substitution of French fries for a Serbian-style fried potato dish.

The style of fried chicken, the cabbage slaw and the hot sauce are European in origin and have become part of the fabric of Barberton culture and cuisine. It is the classic melting pot dish, combining the immigrant experience with an easily recognizable American style of cooking. Former mayor Randy Hart once said—and caused some controversy for doing so—that Barberton should be known for more than just chicken. He missed a valuable point. A later mayor, Robert Genet, said that there are worse things for which Barberton could be known.

Few cities have a food that they can call their own, something that marks them as a special, individualized community. Barberton fried chicken is unique to the city and is a magnet for food fans. That is civic identity at its most basic. When you think of regional foods, a cuisine that is available only in that location, you can come up with only a few examples. Philadelphia has its cheesesteaks, with a rivalry between Pat's and Geno's. Tourists to Philadelphia go out of their way to eat a cheesesteak. New York City has pizza—Ray's or Patsy's—but pizza is available everywhere, with much of it good. New Orleans is a place that you go to eat gumbo or muffulettas, but that food is also available everywhere. Barberton is the only place where you can get that special Serbian fried chicken. Tourists—and some do already—should go to Barberton for fried chicken, just as one would go to Philly for a cheesesteak. It is, in every sense, original. The phrase "The Fried Chicken Capital of the World" is not just a nickname for Barberton, it's a point of pride. As the television show *Food Feuds* has it, "Fried chicken put Barberton on the map."

Chapter Five

BELGRADE GARDENS

We are serving the children and grandchildren of our first customers.
—*Kosta Papich*

L egend has it that when Belgrade Gardens first opened, it did not serve Serbian fried chicken. The fare was simple lunch items, soups and sandwiches. The owner's wife, Smilka Topalsky, cooked on a small kerosene stove in an equally small kitchen in a converted farmhouse. The restaurant originally had seating for thirty-five people. One day, she was cooking some of the recipes she had brought with her from her home in the Banat region of northeastern Yugoslavia. The food she was cooking was to be her family's dinner. Customers at the restaurant, intoxicated by the aroma of paprika and onions, asked what she was cooking. They wanted some of that exotic food. Overnight, a culinary star was born. To this day, the slogan of Belgrade Gardens is "Where the Old World Meets the New."

Smilka was born on September 23, 1894, in Nadalj, Yugoslavia. She and her family immigrated to Barberton when she was thirteen. Manojlo "Mike" Topalsky came to Barberton with his parents from Vojvodina, an autonomous province in northern Serbia, in 1904, when he was twelve years old. Smilka and Mike met and were married in 1925. The *Akron Beacon Journal*'s Lisa Abraham wrote an article about the early days of Smilka's cooking, "Tradition: 80 Years of Lard-Fried Chicken at Belgrade Gardens." In the article, Smilka's daughter Sophia Papich confirms the legend: "Then one day, two businessmen were at the diner, one of whom was the president

HOW DID A LITTLE FARMHOUSE RESTAURANT IN BARBERTON, OHIO GAIN A WORLDWIDE REPUTATION FOR GREAT CHICKEN DINNERS?

Artwork from an article on Belgrade Gardens. *Photo courtesy of Belgrade Gardens.*

of the First National Bank. While they were eating out front, Smilka was in the back, cooking supper for her family. Their noses followed the smell of her cooking, and they asked if they could have what she was making instead of what was offered on the menu. 'My mother was making dinner for us; she was frying chicken and potatoes.'"

When planning to expand a business, impressing the president of the First National Bank is nothing but good news. From that day on, Belgrade Gardens served its signature Serbian chicken dinner. Smilka may have been the first to serve the chicken back as a separate piece; she was the innovator. Although, based on Serbian recipes, Barberton chicken is an American original, a symbol of the immigrant's dream in the new land.

Mike Topalsky's family owned a dairy farm in east Barberton, near the border with Coventry Township. The Alexander Topalsky Dairy Farm delivered milk to Barberton and Coventry residents in a horse-drawn wagon. Following the death of his father, Alexander, Mike, the oldest of twelve siblings, inherited the farm. In the throes of the Great Depression, the family had to sell the place. In 1933, Mike and Smilka rented the old family farm to open what would become the first of the Barberton fried chicken houses, Belgrade Gardens. By 1940, the restaurant was so successful that they were able to buy back the farm.

They paid attention to the landscape, with a big lawn, trees and flower beds. The landscaping was to give the restaurant on old-world look, but it accomplished something else. The grounds and the restaurant's name

Alexander Topalsky's dairy farm, which became home to Belgrade Gardens. *Photo courtesy of Belgrade Gardens.*

caused the people of Barberton to associate chicken with gardens. Three of the chicken houses had "Garden" in their names. There were even chicken pens in the backyard. The chickens were there to provide eggs, not to be entrées.

Pamela Pace wrote to reminisce about the old days at the restaurant: "Belgrade Gardens was the first outing of my life. My parents and sister went there about once a month. I was only a month old in 1949. I remember going [a]round back where the live chickens were in pens." Many children shared that experience.

The restaurant served only one entrée item: chicken and French fries cooked in lard, the cabbage slaw and the hot sauce. Ruth Patterson, who wrote the "Making the Rounds with the Gaddy Gourmet" column in the *Akron Beacon Journal*, claims that Belgrade Gardens was the first Ohio restaurant to specialize in chicken. When diners were seated, the server, generally local women, would count heads and automatically bring the appropriate number of dinners. The one variation from that menu was that the restaurant would substitute applesauce for the hot sauce for children (or for those who did not like spice). By the way, the one major adjustment to the menu involves the hot sauce. Sophia Papich said that the sting of Hungarian hot wax peppers was toned down a bit to suit the customers' sensitive tongues. Children continued to get the applesauce until their palates were ready for the bite of the hot sauce. It was a rite of passage when you graduated from applesauce to hot sauce. The breading of the chicken was as close to perfection as it can get. There was an urban legend that Belgrade Gardens used vanilla wafers for their breading rather than breadcrumbs. The chicken was refrigerated overnight to bind the breading to the meat. The breading forms the all-important crust that seals in juices after the deep frying.

The cost of the original fried chicken dinner was $0.50. To celebrate its fiftieth anniversary, Belgrade Gardens brought back the $0.50 dinner. In the 1950s and '60s, the heyday of the chicken houses, dinners were $1.00 for adults and $0.50 for children. It was not until 1966 that Belgrade Gardens added more menu items. The price of the chicken was raised to $1.25 in 1969. The restaurant was serving more than four thousand dinners a week.

After dinner, children looked forward to getting a Dum-Dum lollipop from the bowl at the cashier's desk. In a major break from tradition, Hopocan Gardens and White House Chicken have replaced Dum-Dums

Belgrade Gardens's original dining room. *Photo courtesy of Belgrade Gardens.*

with Charms Pops. The history of Dum-Dums was featured in an *Akron Beacon Journal* cover story by Mark J. Price. Dum-Dums were created by the Akron Candy Company. The pops, invented in 1924, were named after the Dum Dum expanding bullet, which they somewhat resembled. The bullets were named for a British arsenal in the small town of Dum Dum in the Bengal region of India. In any case, the Dum Dum is an essential part of the Belgrade experience.

The Toplasky family was well connected in the Serbian community of Barberton. Smilka was involved with the Serbian Orthodox Church, the Circle of Serbian Sisters and the Serbian National Federation. Her grandson, and the current general manager of the restaurant, Milos Papich, a fount of knowledge about Serbian history and culture, sings with a Serbian choir. Always a part of the cultural and historical legacy of Barberton, Belgrade Gardens donated $500 to kick-start the campaign by the Barberton Historical Society to restore O.C. Barber's Anna Dean Farm.

Keeping with its community spirit, Belgrade Gardens would deliver meals to hospitals, especially to the Akron-General Medical Center cancer ward. Pharmacy sales reps would treat kids in hospitals to Belgrade Gardens chicken. In the late 1950s, it sold lunches and dinners to all of the workers at the city's factories. Later, Milich's Village Inn had the largest share of that business.

Many of the early employees were members of the Topalsky family. Among the early nonfamily employees were Helen DeVore and Catherine Milich, who would later have their own chicken restaurants. All of the founders of the Barberton Fried Chicken houses are related to Belgrade Gardens, says Milos, by work experience, blood or marriage.

When the Topalskys stepped down (actually, Mike had died in 1951), management was taken up by their son Lewis and their nephew Alex Suboticki. Lewis would say that Belgrade Gardens was "the finest restaurant of its kind in the area." Lewis and Alex ran the restaurant from 1951 until 1963, presiding over its twenty-fifth anniversary. Smilka and Mike's daughter Sophia, a former teacher, had married an electrical engineer named Kosta Papich, who would become president and general manager of Belgrade Gardens Inc., a position he has held for more than fifty years, after Lewis and Alex moved on. He joined the business when Sophia feared that it needed revitalization.

Kosta had been educated at the University of Belgrade during the reign of Marshal Josip Broz Tito, prime minister and minister of foreign affairs. In the early days of Tito's control of postwar Yugoslavia, the government was repressive. In later years, Tito loosened his iron fist slightly, due to pressure

Early workers at Belgrade Gardens. Note Helen Devore on the right. *Photo courtesy of Belgrade Gardens.*

from the United States, Serbian royalists and more liberal, if not necessarily anti-communist, politicians. Two of Kosta's teachers at the university were professors Petrovic and Jolanovic. They had a lasting influence on him and instilled in him a conviction that "whatever you do, do the best you can." One of his professors canceled classes on St. Nicholas Day, a religious holiday somewhat frowned upon by Tito's regime. The entire university waited for a retaliation that never came.

Kosta came to the United States for the first time in 1957. One of his uncles, Walter Papich, had come to America on the RMS *Carpathia*, the ship that rescued *Titanic* survivors. Kosta returned to Yugoslavia for two years but came back to complete his education. He became a permanent U.S. resident in 1959 and continued his studies at the University of Akron. He got a job in electrical engineering at the B.F. Goodrich Company. Kosta has made Thomas Edison's maxim his own. He says, "Genius is 1 percent inspiration and 99 percent perspiration." He left Goodrich to join his wife, Sophia, full-time at Belgrade Gardens.

Being an engineer, Kosta brought his scientific methods to restaurant management. He studied the needs of his customers and learned how to streamline, but not weaken, the restaurant's methods. Belgrade Gardens was expanded to seat 270 people. (It now seats 350.) The restaurant had been remodeled in 1942 to seat 130. Its 150-car parking lot ensures that diners can access the place easily.

Success leads a restaurant to innovation. The Papich family could no longer afford to hand-bread their chicken. It takes more hours to bread by hand than any efficient restaurant could afford. Kosta investigated the use of a breading machine. He went to the other houses to see if one would work for him. He decided on a Stein MB3 machine, which had been partially designed by Bob DeVore of Hopocan Gardens. The Stein is smaller than the one used at the big chains but has better results for a craft restaurant like Belgrade Gardens. Although they switched to an automated system, they are confident that machines will never replace people. It still takes four or five people to run the machine. Now, Belgrade Gardens breads by machine three times a week—a two- or three-day supply.

Kosta even experimented with pressure frying, as the big chains do, but was disappointed in the results. He wanted to make "the product people expect from us."

Kosta stressed the quality of customer service: "Treat your customers with respect. If you respect them, they'll respect you." He came from a large family, and the concept of family and togetherness is a major part of the Belgrade Gardens experience. These are values he passed on to his son Milos, who is now running the operation. In his youth, Milos was learning the trade. He got his start in the breading room when he was eight years old. Milos officially joined the organization in January 1991, when he became the manager of the Belgrade Garden restaurant in Green, Ohio, closer to Canton than to Akron.

Belgrade Gardens now serves about 2,200 chicken dinners a week in Barberton and another 1,300 in Green. In its heyday, it sold 10,000 dinners a week. It currently employs sixty people, thirty-five in Barberton and twenty-five in Green. When economic conditions in Barberton got worse, the Papich family did not cut hours.

Neither did they cut quality. Respondents on Yelp and other crowdsourcing websites claim that Belgrade Gardens is too expensive. It has always been the highest in price. The chickens used to average one to one and a half pounds but now are two to two and a half pounds, which is bigger than most places. Kosta believes that the quality is worth

The Portage Rubber Company, which would later become Seiberling Rubber. *Photo courtesy of the Akron-Summit County Public Library.*

A souvenir postcard of the Diamond Match Company. Barber's decision to relocate his factory to Barberton saved the city following the Panic of 1893. *Photo courtesy of the Akron-Summit County Public Library.*

The Barber Mansion, the fifty-two-room, Beaux-Arts–style home of O.C. Barber, built at a cost of $400,000. *Photo courtesy of the Akron- Summit County Public Library.*

Barn No. 1 and the greenhouses of the Anna Dean Farm are still standing. The Yoder Brothers chrysanthemums were grown here. *Photo courtesy of the author.*

Above: Paprikas, or paprikash, is the national dish of Hungary. The Serbian version is not thickened with sour cream. *Photo courtesy of the author.*

Left: Al's Quality Market, the home of Slovenian and Hungarian sausage. *Photo courtesy of the author.*

Al's display of local beers. Cincinatti's Little Kings Cream Ale has pride of place. *Photo courtesy of the author.*

The Hunky Night sampler plate at the Green Diamond Grille. *Photo courtesy of the author.*

The array of Serbian foods at Belgrade Gardens: *cevapcici*, the chicken lunch, *djuvece* (hot sauce) and the chicken back. *Photo courtesy of James Carney.*

The celebrated hot sauce of Barberton. *Photo courtesy of James Carney.*

Left: The Akron Candy Company's Dum Dum pop, the perfect post–fried chicken treat. *Photo courtesy of the author.*

Below: Maja and Milos Papich, the third-generation owners of Belgrade Gardens. *Photo courtesy of Belgrade Gardens.*

Left: Hoppy, the Hopocan Chicken, greets visitors to Hopocan Gardens. *Photo courtesy of James Carney.*

Below: The entrance to DeVore's Hopocan Gardens. *Photo courtesy of James Carney.*

Above: Brian Canale, vice president of Hopocan Gardens. *Photo courtesy of James Carney.*

Left: The White House Chicken sign faces Wooster Road and the Magic City Shopping Center. *Photo courtesy of James Carney.*

Above: Notice the thickness of the hot sauce at Village Inn. It was once known as "Mike's Special." *Photo courtesy of James Carney.*

Right: The new kid on the Chicken block, Scott Marble, owner of Village Inn Chicken. *Photo courtesy of James Carney.*

Left: Chicken and waffle: a southern dish or Pennsylvania Dutch? *Photo courtesy of the author.*

Below: The Coffee Pot, a Barberton institution, will celebrate one hundred years on Second Avenue in a few years. *Photo courtesy of James Carney.*

Above: The Erie Depot, built by Barber. It is now a sandwich and ice cream shop. *Photo courtesy of the author.*

Below: Historic postcard of Lake Anna, the heart of downtown Barberton. *Public domain.*

The lunch plate from Belgrade Gardens. Note the thickness of the hot sauce. *Courtesy of the author.*

Belgrade Gardens chicken and paprikash. *Photo courtesy of James Carney.*

A postcard of the Barberton Inn. *Public domain.*

Belgrade Gardens slaw, the only one with carrots. *Photo courtesy of the author.*

Above: Panoramic shot of the Piggery, one of the few remaining buildings from O.C. Barber's Anna Dean Farm. *Public domain.*

Below: Postcard featuring an aerial view of the Sieberling Rubber Company. Its closing in 1982 was a major blow to the city. *Public domain.*

Opposite, middle: Joanne Temo's Serbian folk art mural, featuring Eastern European–style dress at Belgrade Gardens. *Photo courtesy of the author.*

Opposite, bottom: Tuscarawas Avenue in downtown Barberton as it once was. *Public domain.*

Aerial View of Main Plant
Seiberling Rubber Company, Barberton, Ohio
With a Close-up of Modern Office Building

TUSCARAWAS AVENUE, BARBERTON, OHIO.

Belgrade Gardens chicken breast and fries. *Courtesy of James Carney.*

White House chicken plate. *Courtesy of the author.*

the price. Belgrade Gardens has a large physical area, a bigger staff and more comfortable surroundings. Anyone in the restaurant business knows that produce and supply prices are rising (even the cost of chicken feed has an effect on an independent restaurant). Belgrade Gardens is committed to delivering quality and value.

Now that margins are tighter, the restaurant feels that the quality—and the price—are worth it. It has a responsibility "to do right by the people before us," as Milos says. He feels that people want something more authentic, more unique. It is a family tradition to have the Sunday chicken dinner. In years past, the line went out to the parking lot after church on Sundays. This was true at all of the chicken houses. Now people attend their children's sporting events and have busy schedules; people no longer have time for family dinners. Still, Belgrade Gardens is holding its own, and the business is stable as it approaches its eighty-fifth anniversary. Tradition still matters.

One of any business's chief assets is its staff. When a restaurant has many long-term employees, they are as much a part of the experience as the food. Rosanda Ivanis (pronounced "Ivanish") is long-termer. She is the establishment's longest-serving cook, having fried chicken for twenty-five years. Server Melinda Waller has worked there for forty-two years. She still calls Milos "Mickey," his childhood nickname. Many of the cooks have been from the Old World. The Belgrade Gardens cooks and servers over the years have included Jokica Tosanovic, Maria Gulic, Maja Rakic, Eva Farkas, Ljubca Mitrovic, Anna Tkalic and Radmilla Djonovic. Anna Anushock headed the kitchen staff from 1942 on. If a stranger should wander into the kitchen of Belgrade Gardens, chances are that Serbian would be the language heard there.

The most-remembered long-term server was Violet Antof, who had been at Belgrade Gardens for almost forty years. She was hired in 1942. Violet is also the godmother of Milos Papich. Randy Martens posted on "Akron, Ohio Memories: "My family rarely went out to dinner in the '50s and '60s but when we did, it was always Belgrade Gardens. I left Akron in the 70s but any time I went back…she was there." Facebook respondents immediately said that it sounded like Violet. Kate Byers said: "Waaayyy back when….a waitress whose name was 'Violet,' would deliver our dinners three or four at a time. She could balance three plates on one forearm and one or two in the other hand. ([A] nd she wasn't young. I always thought her an amazing woman)." Byers later added "[Violet] always brought my father-in-law extra hot sauce."

By the way, Violet's skill with multiple plates is the norm. Waitresses were taught how to carry five plates at a time, generally without losing so much as a fry. Other waitresses were remembered on Facebook: Sandy Fowler and Drew Schoenly. People develop connections not only to restaurants but also to their favorite servers.

Belgrade Gardens always sourced its food from local vendors. In years past, it would get its chicken from McKeever Farm, from producers in nearby Canal Fulton and from DiFeo and Son's Poultry in Akron. DiFeo's is another immigrant success story. Alfonso DiFeo, an Italian immigrant, opened his poultry shop in 1918, selling live chickens. The business grew to be the major poultry wholesaler in the Akron area. Pies come from the Gardner Pie Company in Akron (also GMO-free). The bread crumbs used at Belgrade Gardens and the noodles for the chicken noodle soup come from producers in Cleveland (or from the grocery when the supply runs out, which did happen recently).

Speaking of Belgrade's chicken soup, a later addition to the menu, Pam Pace thinks, "Belgrade has the best chicken soup ever!" Sometimes, varying the menu draws new fans to an old, established restaurant.

Over the years, the restaurant added more items to the menu. A restaurant does not live on fried chicken alone. The most noteworthy addition was chicken paprikash. The dinner is served in a large oval bowl, full of peppery stewed chicken. This is the Serbian version of the dish, not thickened by sour cream. The broth is an onion- and paprika-scented broth that would be ideal on cold and snowy nights. A food writer at the *Akron Beacon Journal* once wrote, "Come for the chicken, stay for the paprikash." Belgrade's panko-coated fish is fried in canola oil, making it one of the best choices for those who do not eat meat or chicken. One diner, misunderstanding the item on the menu, thought that panko was the type of fish served. It is usually pollock.

Keeping with its Serbian roots, Belgrade Gardens also serves beer from the homeland. Yellen pivo, which translates to "deer," has a red deer on its label. It is brewed by Apatin Brewery, a division of Molson in Canada. A light lager, Yellen is the best-selling beer throughout that region of the former Yugoslavia. Lav ("lion") is the second-best-selling beer, brewed by a division of the Danish Carlsberg Group. In years past, beer drinkers could enjoy local beers, like Weidemann's, by the pitcher.

Belgrade Gardens is still located in the old Topalsky farmhouse, although many additions have been made to the existing structure. The large parking lot is to the left, and a long walkway leads to the glass double doors. Inside the doors is a vestibule and waiting area. To your left is a dessert carousel. To the right is an erasable whiteboard where the day's specials are posted.

They also use the board to display merchandise, like the restaurant's T-shirt. Inside the next set of doors is the main waiting room, with a log couch for busy times and a glass case filled with ceramic chickens. Serbian art and newspaper articles are framed and on display around the room. One of the articles is about the year Woodford Elementary students made Christmas decorations for the restaurant. As a result, 403 people—schoolkids, their teachers and the staff—got free lunches at Belgrade Gardens.

The greeter, generally Milos or his wife, Maja, will guide you to one of the smaller dining areas to the left or to the major dining room farther back, decorated with Serbian folk art murals painted by local artist Joanne Temo. Temo is married to the owner of Temo's Candy Company, a Greek-owned business that has been serving chocolates and candied apples in Akron for almost as long as Belgrade Gardens has been frying chicken. The dining room in the Belgrade Gardens satellite restaurant in Green has a mural depicting the Serbs' war with the Turks. Milos loves talking about Serbian history.

To the right of the greeter's stand, past the bar and the necessary rooms, is the Orange Room, Belgrade Gardens' banquet facility. It is called the Orange Room because at one time it had an orange carpet. The rooms at the restaurant are color coded; apart from the Orange Rom, there are the Blue, Red and Green Rooms. The Orange Room is part of the Belgrade legend. One man, Gus Hall, said that his "son and daughter-in-law were married. The rehearsal dinner was to be held at a restaurant that had lost its power." Hall recalled, "I called a number of places and no one could accommodate us. Called Belgrade Gardens and they said they would have a room set up for us in 15 minutes. Now that is service!"

Belgrade Gardens' customers are loyal. Kosta Papich tells a story of the day he was sitting at his desk when his wife called from the restaurant. She urged him to come downstairs. What he found was a man waiting for his carryout order. What made this so unusual was that the man, a loyal Belgrade diner, was from Sewickley, Pennsylvania, more than one hundred miles away. He had paid a cab $152 to take him to his favorite restaurant. Celebrities have eaten at the restaurant: *Laugh-In* comedienne JoAnne Worley, football's Larry Csonka and Bo Schembechler, Senator George Voinovich (whose uncle was forced from Croatia at the age of seventy-five) and Governor Robert Taft. Judith Resnick, who died in the *Challenger* disaster, said, "Your chicken is the best I have tasted anywhere in the country." In the old days, when the United States Postal Service allowed food to be sent through the mail, dinners had been sent to Florida, California, Texas, Washington, Hawaii and Alaska.

During the war in Vietnam, many parents sent Belgrade dinners to their family members stationed in Southeast Asia.

Milos Papich is filled with pride when he talks about Belgrade Gardens and his family history. There is a congeniality among the Barberton fried chicken houses but a sense of competition, too. Milos said: "We know they're out there, that people have an alternative. It reminds us to be on our toes." He knows that he is competing not only with the other chicken houses but also with every restaurant in the area.

He is philosophical about the changing environment in Barberton. When the Rolling Acres Mall opened in 1975, it brought thousands of shoppers to the area. When it closed, the effect was felt by every local business. The mall became a viral phenomenon when pictures of the deserted, crumbling structure appeared on the Internet. "We need to remind people to come here," Milos says.

Restaurants do not have politics, or they should not. Due to Milosevic and the Bosnian War, the situation in the Balkans may have had an impact on the Serbian chicken restaurants. As recently as 2016, a Croatian accused of war crimes was arrested in Barberton. People may have felt uncomfortable going to a restaurant whose culture was in the news in such a brutal fashion. This happened to many Afghani restaurants after 2001. Milos feels that the continued success of Belgrade and the others is "a tribute to a cooking style from a place that is now looked down upon." Chicken knows no boundaries and makes no political judgements.

The restaurant does some advertising to draw customers in, mostly in the *Akron Beacon Journal*. Like most of the other restaurants, it offers coupons or announces specials on its website. However, Belgrade Gardens has benefited from media attention. The restaurant has been featured in *Ohio Magazine*, the *Beacon Journal* (which named it the no. 1 chicken restaurant in Northeastern Ohio) and the *Cleveland Plain Dealer*. *USA Today* named Belgrade Gardens one of the ten best chicken restaurants in the United States in 2003.

The restaurant has been covered in the late *Northern Ohio Live* magazine, *Cook's Country* magazine and Columbus's *Crave* (the article discussed all of the Barberton fried chicken restaurants). In June 2013, *Parade* magazine featured it in its "Summer Escapes" issue. On television, it has been featured on Del Donahue's show on WKYC and on WJW's *P.M. Magazine*. Jane and Michael Stern praised the place on their show *Dining Worth the Drive*. They called it a must-eat and wrote of the restaurant in their books *Roadfood* and *500 Places to Eat Before You Die*.

The biggest splash Belgrade Gardens made in the media was on the Food Network's show *Food Feuds*. In an episode that ran in November 2010,

The prep area at Belgrade Gardens. *Photo courtesy of James Carney.*

Belgrade Gardens was pitted against White House Chicken, the battle for the title "Barberton's Best." The episode was titled "American Feuds," and it focused on regional food rivalries. Two other Akron-area restaurants, Skyway and Swenson's, battled for the "Best Burger" title. Belgrade Gardens won the contest because of the breading, and its golden-brown coating demonstrated frying expertise. The establishment was crowned during a ceremony at Lake Anna. Milos immediately said that it "was a good day for my family."

The honors continued for the original Barberton chicken house. County executive Russ Pry read a declaration naming it Belgrade Gardens Day in Summit County on July 12, 2012. Kosta, Sophia, Maja and an emotional Milos Papich accepted the honor with pride. They deserved the laurels as the custodians of the original version of a true Ohio original.

. . . .

BELGRADE GARDENS, founded July 1933
401 East State Street, Barberton, OH, 44203
belgradegardenschicken.com

Chapter Six

HOPOCAN GARDENS

If the Colonel had our recipe, he would have been a general.
—*Robert DeVore*

The first thing you notice as you drive in to the Hopocan Gardens parking lot is Hoppy, the giant chicken statue that stands near the entranceway. A parking sign warns "Chicken Lover Parking Only. All Others Will Be Fried."

It might come as a surprise to the people who eat at DeVore's Hopocan Gardens regularly, but the DeVores were not the original owners of the restaurant. Even that is not cut and dried. The DeVores did own the building and had leased it to the Hopocan founders.

Two tire builders from Barberton's Seiberling Rubber Company, Joe Palmer and Mirko "Mike" Milich, rented an open-air picnic pavilion owned by William and Helen DeVore. They were joined by Mike's wife, Catherine, better known as Katie. Working with staff of four, they built the restaurant into what it is now. In those days, the chicken dinner cost seventy-five cents.

Joe Palmer reminisced in the *Akron Beacon Journal* in 1978 that although he and Mike had to work long hours at Seiberling during World War II to get the money to open Hopocan Gardens, "we had to work much harder at Hopocan Gardens, but I'm glad I quit Seiberling. I worked there 24 years."

In the early 1960s, the lease was up on the building—an expanded building, not the pavilion. The Palmer/Milich partnership dissolved. Palmer and his new partners Eileen and Roy Johnson pursued other opportunities.

Joe Palmer and Mirko "Mike" Milich, the original owners of Hopocan Gardens. *Photo courtesy of the Barberton Public Library.*

Eileen Johnson had been a cook at the restaurant. They became the owners of Terrace Gardens, which opened one-quarter mile west of Hopocan Gardens. Mike would later open Milich's Village Inn. The Devore family entered and made Hopocan Gardens their own.

Bill DeVore was William Vla when he came to this country. He found that a person with a foreign-sounding name had difficulties finding a job. One day, he saw a boxing poster advertising a bout at the Akron Armory. One of the fighters was Kid DeVore, which Vla thought was a great American name. He adopted the surname DeVore, although he never changed his name legally. Helen, also from the Banat region of Serbia, was a former Belgrade Gardens employee.

In the restaurant's heyday, Hopocan sold three thousand pounds of chicken and two thousand pounds of fries weekly. Dale Milich said that in their glory days you could spot license plates from seventeen states in the Hopocan Gardens parking lot.

Like many of the Barberton fried chicken houses, Hopocan Gardens is a family affair. William's son Robert DeVore was peeling potatoes at thirteen. Robert joined his father in management in 1960 after leaving the service. Today, he is president of Hopocan Gardens Inc. The vice president who oversees operations is Brian A. Canale, the grandson of

The portrait of Helen and William DeVore hangs over the cash register at Hopocan Gardens. *Photo courtesy of the author.*

William and Helen DeVore. Brian also oversees the sister restaurant White House Chicken. He got his start at Hopocan Gardens, breading chicken when he was twelve. Bill DeVore used to take lunches, twenty at a time, to the Babcock and Wilcox plant to sell to the workers there. In later years, Helen would sit at her favorite spot, at the first table near the kitchen, and watch her operation. Her friend Jean Vargo was the manager for twenty-five years; she and her sister Carolyn, also known as Sally, would join Helen at the table.

In 1978, before plants started closing in Barberton, Robert summed up the story of the Barberton fried chicken houses: "If my competition is busy, I'll be busy too....The customer may drive around to find the shortest line, but there's enough business for all of us." Times have changed, and Hopocan has changed with them.

Canale knows his traditions: "We...use the exact same preparation process and the same cooking methods [as the restaurant always had]. The recipe is simply chicken, flour, eggs, unseasoned breadcrumbs, and salt." Hopocan gets its chickens from Gerber's, with some from Canal Fulton Provisions.

He laughingly says that the chickens come eight to a carton. The Amish lads who do the packing can carry four in each hand, with the chicken's feet between their fingers.

The prototype of the Stein Mini Batter Breader for chicken breading was first used here in 1973. Its Process Conveyor Belt was developed by Bob DeVore. Sam Stein Associates Inc. of Sandusky, Ohio, started in 1955 with automated coating machines for restaurants. DeVore saw the potential. With the Stein, Hopocan could bread fifteen thousand pieces of chicken weekly. It would have taken four employees thirty days to accomplish the same feat. An automated breader could save a restaurant $10,000. Hopocan now uses a breading machine by Bettcher, a subsidiary of Stein.

Canale said on *Food Feuds* that they fry their chicken for sixteen minutes at 265 degrees. "Low and slow" is how he describes it. Hopocan tried to add T-bone steaks to the menu, but it proved difficult to teach young chicken cooks how to grill them properly.

Brian Canale also knows marketing. He is the past president of the Akron Area Restaurant Association and a former board member of the Ohio State Restaurant Association. He uses Bellycard.com for promotion and marketing purposes. The app describes itself as "an iPad-based loyalty and marketing platform." Its Hatch technology gathers data for restaurant owners. With the statistics he gets from the website, Canale can do targeted marketing. Some of the news is gratifying, some bothersome. There are few patrons in the eighteen to twenty-four age group, and a small percentage in the coveted twenty-four to thirty group. His clients are older but devoted.

Canale lures customers with promotions, coupons on the restaurant's website and Groupons. The restaurant does some radio underwriting. In the past, it ran spots with the local Cleveland Indians affiliate. It also used to advertise in the Barberton Speedway program. At Christmastime, Hopocan sells a lot of gift certificates, which guarantees solid business in January.

The dining room is the most rustic of the chicken houses, with lots of wooden beams. It looks like a western farmhouse. It is a warm and inviting room, perhaps one of the more comfortable of the chicken houses. Hopocan Gardens has expanded and been remodeled several times. In the 1960s, the DeVores completely modernized the 1940s kitchen without having to close the restaurant. They worked around the existing kitchen. The expanded restaurant is built around the old picnic pavilion. In years past, the restaurant featured a folk-art mural by local artist Pat Mayadovic, a farm scene with cows and some chickens in a pasture. When Hopocan Gardens is next remodeled, Canale hopes to restore the mural.

The restaurant's website touts the banquet hall services: "Hopocan Gardens can cater any party. Weddings, birthdays, graduations....We can serve 100 guests at our location. We have contacts with many banquet halls in the area for larger groups. Bar and Bartender service available." Private party and banquet services, with a catering operation, can keep a restaurant in black ink.

Hopocan Gardens gives back to its community. It hosts the Chicken Open, a golf tournament that benefits the Akron-Canton Regional Food Bank. Its website links to St. Jude's Children's Research Hospital. Like other Barberton fried chicken houses, Hopocan Gardens provides food for the Ronald McDonald House and area hospitals.

One of the oddest things involving Hopocan Gardens, which did not seem to originate with the restaurant, is a series of animated films on YouTube about "DeVore, the Greasy Chicken." Magic Chicken Productions and 427 have posted cartoons that feature DeVore versus Evil Meals (personified by Ronald McDonald), Wendy and the Taco Bell Chihuahua. Whoever posted these amateur films seems to love DeVore's chicken, despite the chicken's nickname.

Restaurants sometimes have problems establishing their own identities, even restaurants that are a part of long-standing traditions. Recently, a new resident in Barberton called Hopocan Gardens for hot-and-sour soup, thinking it was a Chinese restaurant, according to *Akron Beacon Journal* writer David Giffels. The caller probably didn't realize that other nationalities have gardens, too.

On the "Akron, Ohio Memories" Facebook page, Hopocan customer Jan Boyle said: "I live in Indiana now but make a trip back home at least once a year for chicken. I always bring 100 backs home for the freezer and of course hot sauce." Anita Davis, who has worked at Hopocan Gardens for eighteen years, eats the chicken every day. Customer loyalty is what Barberton fried chicken is all about.

. . . .

HOPOCAN GARDENS, founded 1945.
4396 Hopocan Avenue Ext. Barberton, OH, 44203
http://www.hopocangardens.com

Chapter Seven

WHITE HOUSE CHICKEN

*We decided to call it the White House because it was an easy name to remember.
The White House is in the newspapers every day.*
—Al Pavkov

There is a sign at the entrance to the dining area at White House Chicken that reads "Enter as Strangers. Leave as Friends." That sums up eating at all the Barberton fried chicken houses. People come for the food, but the staff and the friendliness of the place give the restaurants a homey feel. It is like a community, sort of like visiting your family. And the Barberton chicken restaurants are like an extended family.

Mary Marinkovich Pavkov worked at Belgrade Gardens. She was a close friend to the Topalskys, so close that she was godmother (*huma* in Serbian) to Mike Topalsky. She had lived on a farm just outside of Barberton, in the area that would later be developed as the Rolling Acres Mall. Following the death of her husband in 1935, Mary opened the Wooster Road Café, across the street from the original site of the National Sewer Pipe Company.

Years later, Mary met and married Louis Pavkov. She then rented the café to someone else. The place became the Playmore Café. Louis lost his leg in an industrial accident in early 1950, which made Mary the primary earner in the family. She took over the café and, in July of that year, opened it as a thirty-seat fried chicken house in the style of Belgrade and Hopocan Gardens. The Pavkovs lived in an apartment above the restaurant. In later years, after she had stepped down from managing

The "Leave as Friends" sign welcomes visitors to White House Chicken. *Photo courtesy of James Carney.*

the restaurant, Mary would open her door and yell instructions to the workers in the kitchen below.

The original staff was the Pavkov family: one son (Al) and five daughters (Olga, Dorothy, Nettie, Mae and Velma). Another son, Milan, would become the superintendent of Barberton schools. Al would eventually take over management. He liked to say that White House Chicken was the only true Barberton fried chicken house. Belgrade Gardens, he thought, was too near Coventry Township. Hopocan, Terrace and Milich's were in Norton. Therefore, White House was the only restaurant to claim a real Barberton address. It is the only one of the chicken houses in the downtown area.

Despite his claim, Al Pavkov and the other chicken house owners worked together. They were like relatives. Al said, "If one restaurant runs out of something, someone else will share what he has and help out."

The proud history of the restaurant graces the White House Chicken menus. *Photo courtesy of James Carney.*

White House Chicken is located on the corner of Wooster Road and West Paige Avenue. The small, two-story building is brick with white siding on the upper lever. The original building, a residence, was white; the bricking came later. Block letters spell out the name of the restaurant on the front and side of the building, but in recent years, the well-lighted red, white and blue chicken logo sign has been on display, hanging above the restaurant's door. Upon entering the restaurant, you come to a small vestibule, where you are greeted by the person at the cash register. There are a few tables on the right, where the "Friends" sign hangs, but most of the seating is in the large dining room to the left. The dining room looks like a large area in someone's home, which in many ways it was. Wood veneer tables and large windows make you feel as if you are at a family reunion or at a reception of some sort. It is that sort of warm yet casual place. Unlike Belgrade, Hopocan and Village Inn Chicken, White House does not serve beer or wine (odd for a place that had once been a bar). The residents appreciate that; they see it as a place for the family, grandma and the kids. However, for some—those who enjoy beer with their chicken—the dry nature is a negative factor.

Like many of the restaurants, White House has a thriving carryout business. In 1978, Pavkov figured, carryout was 50 percent of the restaurant's overall business. As was the tradition among the Barberton fried chicken houses, until postal regulations made it impossible, White House mailed food to chicken fans around the country. Al said: "We've sent chicken dinners to California....Our customers will put [the dinner] on the 11:00 p.m. non-stop flight...for their friends and relatives."

As is also the tradition, restaurant workers view their work as careers, not just as a temporary job. Debi Merl has been at White House for forty years. Sara Terwilliger, who also works the front desk, is the granddaughter of

Eileen Johnson of Hopocan and cofounder of Terrace Gardens, extending the genealogy of chicken houses.

One year, on National Fried Chicken Day (July 6), a Pennsylvania radio station interviewed Merl, the restaurant's manager. It was an unscheduled call, and she spoke with the talk-show host while she took care of customers. The radio station had heard that Barberton was the "Fried Chicken Capital of the World" and called to congratulate the restaurant on that august date. She had no idea what the caller was talking about, but her pride in the Barberton fried chicken tradition was apparent. She described the collegial nature of the restaurants in the area: "All of these people were friends, they worked together until they broke out to open restaurants of their own."

Many Barberton fried chicken fans think that White House makes the best chicken. Jan and Michael Stern wrote about it on www.roadfood.com: "White House is for skin lovers....A chewy spicy, super-savory coat so thick that the meat inside...yields no juice until the envelop is breached." Al Pavkov liked to stress the slow nature of his chicken. The best product takes time. He said that "none of the food is prepared ahead of time here. If you're in a hurry to eat, you best not come in."

A food blogger named Lisa Buie made a tour of the four existing chicken restaurants in a YouTube video, "The Magic City Chicken Tour." She thought White House had the second-best chicken (after Hopocan), but White House made the absolute best slaw. She thought it was sweeter than the rest.

The White House lunch special, white meat or dark? *Photo courtesy of James Carney.*

One of the best stories on hot sauce was found on the "Akron, Ohio Memories" Facebook page. Maggi Snyder told of her family's history: "White House Chicken was our favorite. We started going there when the dinners were $.75. We were poor and lived in the projects and it was a special treat. My Mom almost always had a jar of their hot sauce in her refrigerator after she had gotten a job with the city and could afford it. She would take a large glass jar and have them fill it up with hot sauce and take it home."

This devotion to the hot sauce, and Ms. Snyder's testimony, shows that the identification with a particular chicken house is a prime motivator in making the decision of where to eat. Some people will look at the Barberton fried chicken houses as a variety of choices—White House makes the best chicken, but Belgrade has the best hot sauce, and so on. Others—and this is the majority of Barbertonians—have their own choice for the place they eat exclusively. White House fans are particularly devoted.

One of the framed items adorning the walls of White House is a letter from an anonymous woman. She and her boyfriend had eaten at the restaurant thirty-eight years before but had done a dine-and-dash, running out without paying. Having carried her guilt for years, she sent the letter of apology and a ten-dollar bill to cover the cost of the dinner. "He was a troublemaker," she wrote. A framed card thanks the White House for their kindness. A woman's father was dying, and his last wish was a White House chicken dinner. The restaurant gave the meal to the woman without charge.

Also hanging on the walls of the vestibule of the restaurant is a sign telling carryout customers that the to-go packaging used is environmentally friendly. They use General Harvest Fiber Biodegradable packing materials. Go green and eat fried chicken!

White House Chicken, with seating for 150, is now owned by Robert DeVore and Brian Canale of Hopocan Gardens; they bought it in October 1990. They opened branch locations, some just carryout, in Tallmadge, Green, Wadsworth and Medina. The corporate name is White House Chicken Systems Inc. The system seems to be working for Canale and his restaurant. Like many of the restaurants, White House also sells merchandise—bright blue sports shirts with the chicken logo, scented candles and their proprietary root beer. The root beer, brewed in nearby Cuyahoga Falls, has a strong flavor and a bite to it. It is a must for fans of the soda.

In an interview on WAKR radio, Brian Canale talked about his preparation for the Food Channel's *Food Feuds* program. He was thrilled that the show would coincide with the White House's sixtieth anniversary. He

Give White House Chicken merchandise for Valentine's Day. *Photo courtesy of James Carney.*

The view of White House Chicken from the Magic City Shopping Center. *Photo courtesy of the author.*

mentioned that, despite the same ownership, White House and Hopocan Gardens stick to their original recipes; they do not serve the same exact food. "They're different," Canale said. "That's why each has its own following." The television chef who hosted the show was from Cleveland and remembered Barberton chicken from his youth. He had even tried to replicate the traditional Barberton fried chicken recipe in one of his restaurants. (Reminder: Barberton chicken does not transplant well.)

Canale spoke about the ethnic relationship between Barberton and the former Yugoslavia. If you go to Bosnia right now, he explained, you can get the same dinner they serve here. Despite his Italian last name, Canale remains a Serb through and through, via his grandparents, the DeVores. About the difference in the four existing chicken houses, Canale struck a similar chord: "The recipes [of each of the four] are close to each other.... There is a different taste to each restaurant."

For a special treat, look for the catchy White House Chicken commercial on YouTube. A pop band sings the song extolling the benefits of "farm-fresh chickens raised in Ohio." The kicker is, "Flavor in every little bite." It's fried chicken you can dance to.

Readers of the *Barberton Herald* have named the White House Barberton's Best Chicken for the past twelve years.

. . . .

White House Chicken, founded July 1950
180 Wooster Road North, Barberton, OH 44203
http://www.whitehousechicken.com

Chapter Eight
TERRACE GARDENS

The menus have now all been expanded greatly to satisfy the thousands
of customers who visit the Barberton chicken houses.
—Eileen Johnson

T he Great Barberton Chick-Off was held in Akron in September 1983. An independent group of tasters, comprising University of Akron faculty members, an artist, an investigative journalist and at least one native Barbertonian sampled the food at all five of the chicken houses. Fortunately for later researchers, one of those university people taught math, and he prepared a statistical analysis of the results—quantitative and qualitative proof of the supremacy of Barberton fried chicken. Terrace Gardens was the surprise winner, beating out closest competitors White House and Milich's by five points.

This victory should not have been so surprising. Terrace Gardens was a particularly popular restaurant. One of the reasons for its success was its low prices; it offered what one would expect—the expertly fried chicken, the hot sauce—for less than its competitors. According to *Akron Beacon Journal* food writer Katie Byard, Terrace served more than fifteen thousand people, at fifty cents apiece, during its grand opening weekend. Families appreciated the low price and were loyal customers for years. Terrace Gardens became the chicken house of choice for university students, for the same economic reason. Thrift can be a motivator when one wants to indulge. The large, airy dining room, which could seat five hundred people, featured a mural of Lake Anna on the back wall. One person on the "Akron, Ohio Memories" Facebook page recalled the restaurant having purple walls. That is unconfirmed. Terrace Gardens served no alcohol, which was a plus for the churchgoing families who frequented Terrace every Sunday.

Terrace Gardens was the brainchild of Eileen Johnson and her husband, Roy. In many ways, the history of Terrace Gardens had its start at Hopocan Gardens. The chicken business in Barberton seems almost generational, with someone from one chicken restaurant opening one of her own. Terrace began with Eileen Johnson and Hopocan's Joe Palmer. Johnson had previously owned a small restaurant in the Western Star neighborhood between Barberton and Wadsworth. Later, she became a cook at Hopocan Gardens. Eileen worked hard and learned the chicken trade. The Johnsons bought out the Milich half of Hopocan Gardens in 1953 and became Palmer's partners. Opportunity came their way when the lease expired at Hopocan Gardens and the DeVore family took over the restaurant.

Eileen and Palmer wanted to continue with their own chicken house. They found a location for their new restaurant as part of a nine-acre lot, barely one-fourth of a mile from Hopocan Gardens. It became the home of Terrace Gardens. It was close to the Norton border, but it was as Barberton as they came. Although the dinners were the same as at the other chicken houses, Johnson thought her food was more like home cooking. The new restaurant opened in 1961 and was managed by Eileen and Palmer. When they opened, they wanted to use the Hopocan Gardens name, but the DeVore family had trademarked it.

In 1997, Terrace Gardens became the first of the legendary chicken houses to close its doors. Eileen Johnson was the last of the original owners of the chicken houses. Roy Johnson had died in 1963; Eileen stayed until age and tough economic conditions forced her hand. By that time, the other restaurants had been taken over by later generations of the founding families. She cited the location, hidden from Shannon Avenue on a side street, as a negative factor on business. The site of the restaurant is now the beautiful Barberton West Elementary School, funded in part by the Barberton Community Foundation with money from the sale of Barberton Citizens Hospital.

Terrace Gardens had been an innovator of sorts. It was the first to offer catering services, catering to church groups, Little League teams and Scout troops. It heralded its banquet facilities; the Christian Supper Club met there regularly. Perhaps the most radical departure from the Barberton chicken formula was Johnson's decision to follow the 1970s trend of a salad bar. For

Barberton Elementary
School West at the former
home of Terrace Gardens.
Photo courtesy of the author.

the first time, diet-conscious diners could at least make a small step toward healthy eating. Instead of fries and hot sauce, a diner could have the chicken with a side of salad, or, worse yet, they could skip the chicken and just go for a healthy green dinner. It opened new possibilities for Terrace, and the owners did see an increase in customers.

Situated as it was so close to Hopocan Gardens, and Milich's Village Inn, the competition heated up for Terrace Gardens. With the financial downturn that Barberton had taken after the closing of the Seiberling plant and other industries, Terrace Gardens could not maintain its level of innovation. It became a symbol of the fading of a beloved tradition. Johnson put some of the blame on the lengthy cooking time of the fresh chicken. "People are in a hurry these days," she told Byard.

Many things have not changed since the Great Barberton Chick-Off. Respondents to a query about the best Barberton fried chicken on the "Akron, Ohio Memories" page gave Terrace a scant five votes, placing it in last place. Yet, for a restaurant that has been closed for twenty years, those are some strong memories.

. . . .

TERRACE GARDENS, founded October 19, 1961;
closed December 18, 1997
228 Hillsdale Road, Barberton, OH 44203

Chapter Nine

MILICH'S VILLAGE INN AND VILLAGE INN CHICKEN

You are the caretaker of something that has and will be here for decades to come.
—Scott Marble

As stated earlier, Milich's Village Inn was founded by Mirko (Mike) and Katie (Catherine) Milich, the former co-owners of Hopocan Gardens. The Milich family had sold their share of that business to the Johnsons and the Palmers in 1955. The Miliches were born in the former Yugoslavia and were married in December 1914. Katie had started out working at the Diamond Match Company at eight cents an hour. Owning her own restaurant was like a dream come true. The Milich family was active in the Serbian Orthodox Church that many of the owners of the chicken houses attended.

Technically, the separation agreement with the Palmers and the Johnsons forbade them from opening a restaurant so near Hopocan Gardens. However, they found a great location in Norton at the former Hagey grocery store on Cleveland-Massillon Road. Although not technically in Barberton, it is a major part of the tradition. It was slightly less than a mile from Hopocan Gardens. Enter the Milich's son Rick, who joined them in opening the new place; he was not subject to the separation agreement and could open the place under his name. Richard had also worked at Hopocan. Then Mike, Kate and Rick were joined by another son, Perry.

The building itself is midcentury modern, with large plate-glass windows that provide plenty of natural light. Some might describe the architectural style as midcentury blah. It is utilitarian and bunker-like, but you go to Village Inn for

Left: The Village Inn Chicken welcome mat greets diners. *Photo courtesy of the author.*

Below: The central dining room at Village Inn Chicken. *Photo courtesy of James Carney.*

chicken, not for aesthetics. There is a large waiting area in the foyer decorated with chicken art. An orange and white sign to the right of the restaurant reads "Dinners to Go"; the door leads to another waiting area, decorated with newspaper clippings and a poster heralding the fifty-year anniversary of the state championship of the Barberton High School varsity football team.

Much of the Milich family worked at the Village Inn. The Milich's offspring were Geraldine, Perry, Rick, Dale and Diana, also known as Aunt Dode. On New Year's Eve, Milich's Village Inn would host a party, with the family working as the serving staff. There was free sauerkraut and pork, the traditional New Year's dish of the Pennsylvania Dutch. In the Great Lakes region, sauerkraut and pork is eaten on New Year's Day for good luck. How far that tradition has expanded would be worthy of further study. Southerners eat black-eyed peas on the holiday.

The restaurant had immediate appeal to west-siders and Seiberling employees. PPG overtime employees would get a free Village Inn dinner from their bosses as part of their compensation. The plant supervisor would do a head count, and a security guard would pick up the dinners.

John Menches of Menches Bros. Restaurant has been a fan of the Village Inn since the mid-1960s. The Menches brothers, Charles and Frank, are considered by some to be the inventors of the hamburger—and the ice cream cone as well.

Rick and his brother Dale bought their father's share of the business in 1970. Dale Milich would be the longtime head of the restaurant. He had gotten out of the service and returned to Barberton with his British wife, Bellamy. Dale had also been on the board of education, like White House Chicken's Milan Pavkov. Dale described his father's history: "[My father] said the first day the restaurant made $100 clear, he'd quit Seiberling." He quit Seiberling, and the restaurant took off. Mike died in 1979, and Katie followed in 1981. At that time, the restaurant was making far more than $100 a day. In its heyday, Milich's was serving one thousand dinners a day. In 2001, dinner cost $5.70, still a tremendous bargain. They claim to have served one-quarter of a ton of chicken annually. The restaurant employed sixty people. In the restaurant's final years, Milich's was overseen by Christine Milich Williams, the grand-granddaughter of the founders, and her husband, Blake.

Milich's was originally a 2,400-square-foot room with seating for 160. The South Room, which now serves as a banquet room, was added in 1957, with an additional 300 seats. Another expansion in 1967, the Window section, added 100 seats. The restaurant was redecorated in 1965, when it added a food storage area and expanded the food prep area. This gave the cooks another much-needed 10,000 square feet. The Miliches bricked the exterior in 1969. A 1986 redecoration added another 8,000 square feet.

When you enter the restaurant and stand on the bright red welcome mat that leads to the dining room, the effect can be overwhelming. It is a cavernous space, filled with Formica tables. It looks like a super-sized dining hall at a university. The large windows facing Cleveland-Massillon Road illuminate the entire space.

Dale Milich once tried to open a similar restaurant elsewhere. He found that his customers did not want to wait for their dinners. It is a rule that Barberton fried chicken is cooked to order. The restaurant's menu points out, "Please allow up to 30 mins on weekdays & up to 60 mins on weekends for fresh hot dinners." This is one of the reasons that the Barberton fried chicken experience does not transplant easily. It also explains why younger diners, used to immediate fast-food gratification, don't embrace the Barberton chicken houses as aggressively.

People who eat at the restaurant form attachments to the staff. Denise Marie Ivey-Abbott remembered that her ex-father-in-law, Bob "Beau" Shuber, was an assistant manager at Milich's after he retired: "[He] was a very rare gem, always had a smile." Waitress Cindy Parsons has been at the Village Inn, in both of its incarnations, for thirty-seven years. Another long-term employee, Connie Short, has been a server at Village Inn, both incarnations, for twenty years.

The Village Inn is well remembered by diners in the area and those who have left. Jean Worthington had moved away from Akron in the '70s. Returning years later, she noticed the new roof and upgrades to the building. "It was as good as I remembered...love the hot sauce and coleslaw." That hot sauce, by the way, is a different, special recipe, created by Katie decades before. New owner Scott Marble guards that recipe—all his recipes, in fact—strenuously. In the early days of Milich's, the hot sauce was known as "Mike's Special." No one could pronounce *djuvice* properly.

Perry Clark said that "[his] father used to take his family of thirteen to Milich's for as long as I can remember for those special occasions (birthdays, graduations, first communions, etc.). As the...family grew to include his children's spouse and his grandkids, my dad would treat the whole family about 70 people." The best reminiscence, though, comes from Darlene Lewis: "When I was a little girl I left my baby doll behind at Village Inn, they never found it and the Miliches bought me a new one and gave it to me."

As in the case of all the Barberton restaurants, the Village Inn sources its food locally. Relatives Ivan and Mildred Milich founded the Faultless Bakery. The chickens came from Case Farms in Holmes County (and now Gerber's

Amish Chicken). Produce now comes from Kalain Produce Inc. in Uniontown. A new dessert selection comes from the Gardner Pie Company of Akron and Leach's Meats and Sweets of Barberton, long-standing local businesses.

Becky Musser was the cook at Milich's for thirty-five years. In an article by the *Beacon Journal's* Katie Byard, she remembered peeling 250 pounds of onions a week. "I can do it my sleep," she said. The restaurant shipped chicken dinners to Florida, Colorado and California until postal regulations put an end to the practice. Musser said that it was very expensive to the customer. Many customers, though, would pay the fee to get their favorite fried chicken.

Robert L. Smith wrote in the *Cleveland Plain Dealer Magazine:* "Milich's has a consistency that's almost religious. Deep-fried cultural touchstones in a city comforted to know that the more things change, the more Barberton stays the same." Jeanne Kaplan recalled that the Village Inn had the best chocolate milk in the world.

Rikki Milich Neubecker, Dale and Bellamy's daughter, never worked at the restaurant but had some stories to tell. When her parents retired, they moved to Strongsville, closer to Cleveland than to Barberton. They asked their new neighbors for a restaurant recommendation, and the neighbors told them it was worth the drive to eat at Milich's Village Inn.

Ron Kern, the son of Velma Pavkov, had been a manager at both White House and Milich's Village Inn. This was after he had closed his own chicken restaurant in Canton. He was running the restaurant in its final days, with Christine and Blake Williams.

Milich's Village Inn closed its doors in 2014. It was a family decision and not dictated by the business climate. Milich's found a new owner in Scott Marble, who rechristened it Village Inn Chicken in 2015.

Scott Marble had gotten his start in the food business at an early age. His first job was at his father's Dairy Queen in Cuyahoga Falls, in the North Hill neighborhood, home to many Italian immigrant families. Even as the new kid on the Barberton fried chicken block, he has known some of his customers for more than thirty years. Prior to buying Milich's, Marble had owned the Handel's Ice Cream franchised store in Alliance. In 1945, Alice Handel began selling ice cream in her husband's gas station in Youngstown. She expanded her business and now has locations in seven states.

When he took over the business, Marble got this bit of advice from the Milich family: "The customer knows best." He knows that more is resting on his shoulders than the success of a business. He is facing expectations and traditions. "Village Inn Chicken is continuing to carry on the same great traditions of what is known as 'Barberton Chicken,'" he has said.

Ex-cook Glen "Cookie" Cook had been frying chicken for twenty-one years. He would cook ten dinners at once in his fryer. Unlike the other restaurants, Village Inn cooks its fries in peanut oil. Cookie used to run specials, sometimes paprikash. The restaurant still offers paprikash dumplings on its regular menu. He said that his least favorite thing to cook is liver and onions, and he dropped it from the menu. Anyone who has ever cooked liver knows that timing is important. Cookie could time the chicken to the second; liver requires too much attention.

Now the head cook is Jason Sammons, who has been working in kitchens his entire career. He got his start at the popular Parasson's Italian Restaurant chain. A chart taped above the chicken fryer tells the exact frying time for each piece, from six to fifteen minutes. Sammons, like Cookie before him, can perform his duties by instinct, without relying on the chart

The restaurant has an extensive fish menu: breaded walleye, pollock, pike, Great Lakes yellow perch and cod. In a heavily Catholic area, fish is still a major dinner item on Fridays.

Catering and the banquet facilities bring in good revenue. The Barberton High School class of 1954 recently held a reunion in the South Room. Most of them had been eating at Village Inn all their lives. Village Inn's well-guarded hot sauce is a popular catering item. "It's great homemade comfort food," says Marble.

Village Inn Chicken is still trying to establish itself. Once articles in the papers say that a restaurant is closing, it is hard to remind people that a new one has opened in its place. Larry Carver of Copley had been a fan of Milich's Village Inn since the 1950s. Days after undergoing surgery at the Cleveland Clinic, he was at the to-go counter at Village Inn Chicken. He had heard that the restaurant had closed but was thrilled when he drove by and saw cars in the parking lot. He wanted to enjoy the fried chicken that he had been raised on.

Village Inn Chicken, now with a staff of twenty-four, runs website coupon promotions and spots on local radio stations to remind area fried chicken lovers that, as its website says, "The Tradition Continues."

. . . .

MILICH'S VILLAGE INN, founded 1955; closed 2014; reopened 2015
VILLAGE INN CHICKEN, founded 2015
4444 Cleve-Massillon Road, Norton, OH 44203
https://www.villageinnchicken.com

Chapter Ten

MACKO'S RESTAURANT

When I was really little we used to go to a place most people never heard of
called Macko's. It was great Barberton chicken.
—Fran Tramonte, "Akron, Ohio Memories" Facebook page

A woman named Doris Webb used to tell her children that Macko's was the best fried chicken house in Barberton. She had worked there as a server and said that their hot sauce was the best in town. The sons and daughters of Doris Webb had heard these stories for years but could never find proof of the restaurant's existence. That seems to be the case with many people in the Akron-Barberton area.

Macko's Restaurant is the long-lost sixth Barberton fried chicken house, although it is known better as a full-service restaurant and bar. Macko's is never grouped with the five famous Barberton chicken houses, but there are reasons why it should be in that crowd. There are reasons why it should not be, too.

Let's start with the reasons for Macko's exclusion. The five Macko brothers were Slovak, not Serbian. The five major chicken restaurants were opened by people who could trace their roots to the former Yugoslavia. The Mackos were of Czech descent. Their people came from Ludrovna, a village in the northern Zilina region of Slovakia. The family was active in Saints Cyril and Methodius Catholic Church and the Slovak Catholic Sokol Assembly 167 (commonly known as the Sokol Center).

The major difference between the restaurants was that Macko's fried its chicken and fish in Primex, a vegetable-based shortening developed by

Macko's Motel. *Photo courtesy of Sue Macko Cianciola.*

Proctor & Gamble. The five chicken houses continued to fry in lard; it is their trademark, so to speak. Primex, although no longer a Proctor and Gamble product, is still used as a frying oil by many restaurants.

Speaking of Proctor & Gamble, it was also the creator of Crisco, the first commercially available vegetable shortening. According to Joan Nathan's *Jewish Cooking in America*, Proctor & Gamble advertised Crisco as the product the "Hebrew Race had been waiting 4,000 years [for]." It remains to be said that, due to the use of lard at the other chicken houses, religious Jews were not able to eat there.

The reason Macko's is, in many ways, the sixth venerable Barberton chicken house is that the chicken dinners it served was the same food served at the big five—fried chicken, slaw, hot sauce and French fries. In later years Macko's became more known for its fried fish dinners, but the traditional Barberton chicken dinner was on offer there since the early 1950s.

The Macko brothers were a commercial powerhouse in themselves. They opened Macko's Restaurant, Macko Towing Company, Macko's Motel and Macko's Sporting Goods. One of the brothers, Walter, later opened a Macko's Restaurant in Titusville, Florida, after he retired to the South. Macko senior, the father, had died in a mill accident just twelve hours after Joe's birth, and the family had to fend for themselves, which might explain their drive.

The Macko family. *Photo courtesy of Sue Macko Cianciola.*

There were five Macko brothers: Anthony, Joseph, Hilary, Walter and Larry. Larry, Tony and Joe had been in the navy during World War II. The family members remained nautical and were dedicated fishermen. Joe named a boat for Karen, one of his daughters, and all the brothers loved being on the water. An article in the *Akron Beacon Journal* by Bill Girgash, "Are Your Nerves Frayed? Then Relax with Fishing Mackos," profiled the brothers. They claim to have caught something like a quarter of a million fish. When on Lake Erie, if they caught only fifty or sixty fish, it was a bad day. Sue Macko Cianciola is one of Joe's daughters. She remembers that "Joe fried either perch or bluegill every Friday until he passed away in 1994. He'd catch the fish every day."

The fish was popular at the restaurant. It had an all-you-can-eat fish dinner on Friday nights, strategically timed to coincide with Barberton High football games, and on Mondays a smelt happy hour. Some diners seem to remember a bluegill dinner special, too. However, fried chicken was the biggest success. One loyal patron, Sandy Emerick, remembers "picking up the carry out boxes around the back [through] a wooden screen door and you went right in to the kitchen!…There were mounds of floured chicken." Emerick also remembers her neighbor Jennie Strimmel cooking at Macko's.

That screen door in the back of the restaurant was the take-out department, and it strikes many chords in the memories of the

Barbertonians who ate there. Marilyn Dickel, who is a volunteer at the Barberton Public Library, was a west-sider, which means that she lived near Macko's. She never went to the White House or Belgrade Gardens, as they were on the east side (roughly two to four miles away). The first thing she recalled was that screen door, as did Dwight Gaskill, although his description was not so flattering. Flies were mentioned. Gaskill, though, was a big fan of Macko's perch and confirmed that its hot sauce and slaw were similar to that of the other chicken houses. Gaskill shared his experiences at Macko's while waiting for his carryout lunch at Belgrade Gardens, by the way.

In many ways, Macko's does fit in with the other, more well-known Barberton fried chicken restaurants. It hand-breaded its chicken, hand-cut the French fries and onion rings and followed its own hot sauce secret formula. In the summer months, when the farms and gardens were active, it used fresh peppers. If it is not betraying any secrets, red pepper flakes were used when fresh peppers were not available. The restaurant got its bread from Barberton's Faultless Bakery. Macko's fried chicken was so well loved that Joe, who was also a pilot, once flew a bucket of the chicken to a Barberton transplant in Alabama.

The Macko businesses were family owned and family centric. At the Macko Motel, which opened in 1957, there was a strict policy. It did not want to get a reputation as one of those types of motels. When the PGA's World Series of Golf was held at nearby Firestone Country Club, some of the pro golfers would stay at Macko's. Sisters Kathleen and Bernadine Macko would babysit the children of Billy "Buffalo Bill" Casper and Bob Goalby when they were off at the tournament. Norton Avenue, the former Route 224, had once been a major thoroughfare. When traffic patterns changed, the motel was forced to close.

Macko's Restaurant added a bar in 1972. It lost some of its churchgoing clientele but gained new customers. It added more dishes to the menu, including frog legs, which, we are told, taste like chicken.

Any restaurant needs to have connections with its community. The Macko's banquet room hosted area bowling leagues (the Sokol Center has a bowling alley in its basement) and wedding parties. Saint Augustine's Cub Scout troop held its annual Blue and Gold Banquet there in the 1960s.

People on the "Akron, Ohio Memories" Facebook page had warm feelings toward Macko's. Roger Reid has a memory that involves two Macko businesses: "My best friend Howard 'Bub' Carl, and I worked [at the restaurant] into the wee hours on Friday nights peeling potatoes and eyeing potatoes for the fries. Several 40-gallon stainless steel vats full." Reid

A holiday celebration at Macko's. *Photo courtesy of Sue Macko Cianciola.*

saved enough from his wages to buy his first shotgun at Macko's Sporting Goods.

A recent post on the "Barberton Fried Chicken" page about Macko's got more responses than any of the other chicken houses. Macko's may be gone, but the memory lives on.

Macko's closed in 1982. Sue Macko Cianciola endowed a scholarship through the Barberton Community Foundation. Her late husband, Donato (Danny), was the son of Frank Cianciola, who ran Cianciola and Son Grocery in Akron. Donata Cianciola was neither Slovak nor Slovenian. The grocery, now known as Cianciola's, continued under the management of Joe Macko's daughters Karen and Sue. The scholarship in Danny's name is open to those in food service and/or hotel management who want to pursue careers. The award states: "In honor of a Parent and Late Husband." This is a fine tribute to a family, to a restaurant and to the Barberton community.

. . . .

MACKO'S RESTAURANT, founded 1948; closed 1982
635 Norton Avenue, Barberton, OH 44203

Chapter Eleven

CHICKENFEST!

It may be a bad couple of days for chickens…
—Barberton Herald, *1988*

I t would make sense that a city that has such a definable signature dish would want to celebrate it. It took the United Way to bring together Barbertonians, fried chickens and community events. The United Way saw Barberton fried chicken as the ideal partner to kick off its fall campaign. Chickenfest! ran from 1988 until the late '90s. Cleveland has its annual Rib Burn Off. Akron has the National Hamburger Festival. One restaurateur wanted to know why Barberton did not have a chicken fry-off. This festival was a move in the direction of recognizing Barberton fried chicken.

Jerilyn Ferguson chaired the first Chickenfest! and would chair many more. Her description in the *Barberton Herald* was, "For Barberton, this just seems like the right thing to do.…There are two goals: to hitchhike onto the United Way's community-wide involvement and to have a celebration of the entire city." The Barberton area United Way served the city, Norton and Doylestown. It hoped to kick off its half-million-dollar campaign with Chickenfest! The goal was to gather restaurants, community organizations and nonprofits, arts and crafts displays and people who loved fried chicken and supported charities. Ferguson did not specifically mention fried chicken in her comments, but it was a rule that chicken was the only meat that could be served at the fest.

The United Way's Norma Benton and Mary Russell (as the Barberton Chicken) at Chickenfest! *Photo courtesy of the Barberton Public Library.*

The first festival was held on September 16 and 17, 1988, at Lake Anna Park. It was set up on West Park Street between Third and Sixth Streets Northwest, near the gazebo. The *Barberton Herald* said that Chickenfest! '88, was bad for chickens "but good…for those who like their poultry as only area chicken houses can make it." It was a community event, with area restaurants and organizations joining in on the fun. Belgrade Gardens, Hopocan Gardens and Milich's Village Inn participated, along with Fa-Ray's family restaurant (of the broasted chicken tradition) and Peachtree Southern Kitchen.

Peachtree was a sort of oddball in the mix. It was not located in Barberton, but in Hudson. It served the traditional southern, not Serbian, fried chicken. It also did not serve hot sauce. However, Chickenfest! was about community, an all-inclusive community. Even Kentucky Fried Chicken participated in the fourth Chickenfest! in 1992.

The Barberton Band Boosters built a mock school cafeteria and displayed the motto "School Chicken Is Cool." Music and entertainment ran continuously. Performers included Barberton's "Polka King," Frankie Spetich; the Fabulous Flashbacks (a 1950s doo-wop group); and the Matt Shaffer Band. German bands, barbershop groups, the Norton Grand Squares and the Wadsworth Swinging Squares joined in. The Barberton Elks Club set up a beer garden. The Kiwanis Club sold nachos.

Frankie Spetich, by the way, was a big name in Barberton. He wanted to be an all-American and somewhat downplayed his Slovenian heritage. He sang with a Slovenian choir before creating his own polka band in 1941. The Frankie Spetich Orchestra performed for the next sixty years. Spetich was a musical superstar, a big draw for Chickenfest!. In 1999, he was inducted into the National Cleveland-Style Polka Hall of Fame.

The entire downtown area was decorated for Chickenfest!. Banners were draped across the streets. The *Herald* supported it. The inaugural fest drew six thousand, but the second year drew more than ten thousand. Barley's restaurant served kabobs at the second fest, which were a hit, according to the newspaper. Event chair Jerilyn Ferguson was more focused in her statements to the paper: "This is not a money raising event, as there is no admission charge. We just want people to have a good time and bring attention to the United Way." A Barberton High Magics victory had people in a party mood, and, as the *Herald* said, "the tempting aroma of the chicken capital of the world's house specialty drew them in."

The 1989 Chickenfest! added events, including a Best Chicken Joke contest, a chicken-calling competition, the Chicken Shoot (dunking rubber chickens into a basketball hoop), the celebrated Chicken Dance and an egg toss. Subsequent Chickenfests! had no shortage of activities. There was Cluck-Cluck Golf (using hard-boiled eggs as golf balls) and Fowl Shooting (again, dunking rubber chickens into a hoop). More physical activities were a Velcro wall and the Chick-O-Lympics, described as "a quasi-athletic event." The Red Cross's Blood Mobile collected donations, and the Barberton Fire Department gave tours of its new fire safety house. The United Way collected at least $1,500 free and clear at the annual event.

The Chickenfest! joke contest was covered by the *Akron Beacon Journal's* Stuart Warner. Someone used the Gay Nineties minstrel quip, "The chicken is an animal we eat before it's born and after it's dead." Warner's article had the headline "It's Chickenfest Time, Lame Yolks and All."

Some practical jokers dropped off a dozen live chickens at Lake Anna Park the night before Chickenfest! opened. The chickens huddled, terrified, under a table. The *Herald* reported that "the jittery white birds looked like they wanted to cross to the other side of the road, away from Chickenfest."

The third festival, in 1991, added a costumed character. The United Way's Jackie Muffet was one of the people who appeared as the Barberton Chicken. More events were added, one of which was the Chicken Coop Jail Cell. You would issue a warrant, which cost one dollar, to lock up someone you knew, who then had to pay a one-dollar bail to get out (or serve five minutes of hard time), A Best Chicken Leg competition was added, too. Whether this was for best culinary skills or shapeliest anatomy was not made clear. There was a car show, and a Golden Egg Award was given.

The 1991 Chickenfest! also marked Barberton's centennial. The United Way float in the Labor Day parade, as a reminder of the festival, featured the city's fried chicken houses. One of the floats at that centennial parade paid tribute to the Petticoat Thief, one of the great Barberton mysteries. At the turn of the last century, someone was stealing women's undergarments

A Belgrade Gardens employee at Chickenfest! *Photo courtesy of the Barberton Public Library.*

from houses and clotheslines. The thief had a fondness for silk. The suspect was never apprehended, although a recent *Barberton Herald* article may have solved the case. One hundred years later, the town still celebrates its odd characters and unsolved crimes.

Over the years, the Barberton restaurants worked alongside and were in competition with their rivals at the fest. The restaurants were known to survey one another's lines. In 1997, the tenth fest, Hopocan served 1,600 people. Belgrade Gardens manager Linda Cockrell said it served between 700 and 800 people. Dale Milich said he had 1,000 diners. Many who ate at Chickenfest! were first-timers. When asked about the food, Bob DeVore said, "if you're worried about cholesterol, Honey, you won't eat Barberton chicken."

Brenda Farrell, the executive director of Barberton Area United Way in later years, stressed the importance of Chickenfest! "It's a way of saying thank you back to the community for their support....Since Barberton is the chicken capital of the world, we chose to organize a festival around that theme."

By 1994, the seventh year, newspaper coverage began to lighten up. Although the tenth Chickenfest!, in 1997, drew ten thousand attendees, the crowds had been fluctuating. The United Way called an end to Chickenfest! shortly thereafter.

Perhaps a scandal at the national United Way headquarters may have dampened some of the enthusiasm for Chickenfest!. William Aramony had been the CEO of the organization for twenty years. He was convicted in 1995 by the U.S. District Court of Virginia on "23 counts of conspiracy to defraud, mail fraud, wire fraud, transportation of fraudulently acquired property, engaging in monetary transactions in unlawful activity, filing false tax returns and aiding in the filing of false tax returns," according to Wikipedia. Money laundering charges were dismissed. When Aramony was sentenced to seven years in prison, the United Way lost some luster and a great deal of support.

The United Way kept the name Chickenfest!, and the city cannot use it without the organization's permission. Mayor Bill Judge would like to see a similar celebration return, a tribute to Barberton's history and cuisine. He likes the name Chick-A-Palooza.

Chapter Twelve

THE RIVALS OF BARBERTON FRIED CHICKEN

OTHER REGIONAL FRIED CHICKEN HOUSES

Frankenmuth sells as much as all of the
[Barberton] chicken houses put together.
—Dale Milich

Barberton is known as "The Fried Chicken Capital of the World" or sometimes "The Chicken Capital of the World." For the people of Northeastern Ohio, this is indisputable. For some in other regions, such as the southern convert John T. Edge, Barberton's claim is valid. Yet, as stated many times before, the American South is still viewed as the home of fried chicken. There are, however, many restaurants with devoted followings in other parts of the country—those who aspire to wrest the crown from Barberton.

Fried chicken was not always as commonplace as it is today. Prior to World War II, chicken was one of the more expensive meats, something to be eaten only on special occasions. When chicken was recognized as a lower-fat, and easily raised, source of protein for American soldiers abroad, it rose in stature as a food source. With the increased production, and with more people getting used to eating it, chicken became a regular item on menus and tables. Edge says that fried chicken "is at once a totem of tradition and a lowest-common-denominator lunch."

Wikipedia tell us that nineteenth-century hog production, which yielded large quantities of lard, and the invention of the cast-iron skillet, led to the popularity of fried food. Emelyn Rude's *Tastes like Chicken* tells us that in the

Carolinas the slave code was revised, making it illegal for slaves to own hogs or cattle. But chickens were allowed. Slaves were able to capitalize on the one resource available to them. In the eighteenth and nineteenth centuries, the intersection of two major roads in Gordonsville, Virginia, made it a popular travelers' rest. George Washington, Thomas Jefferson and James Monroe had all stopped at the Gordonsville tavern. In the middle of the nineteenth century, slaves would sell fried chicken from the railroad platform. A back sold for five cents; legs or breasts went for fifteen cents. The legs became the best seller. Gordonsville fried chicken became so popular that travelers would reroute to get chicken dinners there. The slaves were able to make money from this enterprise. In some cases, they earned enough to buy their freedom.

Two styles of fried chicken developed in that part of the country. Virginia fried chicken, attributed to Mrs. Mary Randolph, was fried in a deep pot of boiling lard, as it is in Barberton. Randolph, a distant relative of Jefferson, ran a boardinghouse in Richmond. Her 1824 book *The Virginia House-Wife* was the first regional cookbook published in America. Randolph, whose food preparation was mostly done by slaves, included the culinary traditions of Africa, Latin America and other cultures in her book. Curry was a popular dish of the day, one she helped popularize.

Chicken Maryland is the other southern style of frying chicken. The major differences between Virginia chicken and Chicken Maryland were that the latter is marinated in buttermilk and served with a cream sauce. Virginia is served in its unadorned fried coating. Chicken Maryland is fried in just a few inches of oil; it is not deep fried. It is covered after browning and allowed to steam. The later style of broasting chicken also involves steaming. Chicken Maryland was popular enough to be featured by master chef Georges August Escoffier in one of his cookbooks. Chicken à la Maryland was served—to first-class passengers, of course—on the *Titanic*.

The cookbook published as *The Way to a Man's Heart*, but more commonly known as *The Settlement Cookbook*, was a fundraising tool for the Settlement House in Milwaukee, Wisconsin. The book was compiled by Mrs. Simon Kander and Mrs. Henry Schoenfeld. Kander, whose own name was Lizzie Black Kander, had helped found the Settlement House to provide support and education for recent immigrants, mostly Jewish, from Europe. It may have been the first cookbook for and by Europeans to be published in this country. As chicken was still considered an expensive feast, a splurge, the cookbook contains only one chicken recipe, and a fairly traditional one at that. It does contain two recipes for making mock chicken and duck out of veal.

For many people, fried chicken means the food of one of the national chains. Church's, which may have had an outlet near downtown Barberton, just a few blocks from White House Chicken, is one of the majors. There is even El Pollo Loco, which specializes in Mexican grilled chicken. This calls to mind Los Pollos Hermanos, the restaurant featured on the television show *Breaking Bad*.

Kentucky Fried Chicken, now known universally as KFC, and Popeye's are two of the biggest fried chicken chains. They have their adherents, even in Barberton. KFC's headquarters is in Louisville, but it got its start in 1930 in the small town of Corbin. Harland Sanders, who had learned to cook at an early age, bought a service station. He started to sell his special fried chicken to travelers on Route 25. He expanded but later sold his restaurant and traveled the country selling chicken franchises. Today, the chain, now owned by the Yum! Brands Corporation, has tens of thousands of restaurants around the globe. Al Copeland founded Popeye's in New Orleans. He named it after Gene Hackman's character in *The French Connection*. No cartoon sailors were involved. The restaurant's test kitchen is in Atlanta, but the chain is known for its Louisiana hot chicken. Popeye's has fans among cooking professionals. James Beard Award winner Wylie Dufresne, whose wd-50 was a well-regarded food mecca in New York, served Popeye's fried chicken at his wedding. Dufresne, by the way, is not a southerner; he's from Rhode Island.

Most histories of fried chicken will tell you that slaves, who were permitted to raise chickens, cooked their birds in their native spices, especially chilies. Randolph mentioned this in her cookbook. It became part of the southern heritage, especially among southerners of African extraction, to spice it up a bit. Recently, KFC has started advertising its new Nashville Hot, based on a popular southern variation on fried chicken. Popeye's had been hot and spicy since its inception, but both chains borrowed from an older tradition. A newer player in the spicy chicken business is Louisiana Famous Fried Chicken, which has a store not far from Barberton

The Nashville recipe that KFC alludes to is best summed up at Prince's Hot Chicken Shack, which has been serving fried chicken with varying levels of heat since the 1930s. Founder Thornton Prince, the story has it, was a womanizer who enjoyed a bit of wildness. His girlfriend, angered at his nights out, decided to punish him by adding the juice of a hot pepper and other hot spices to his fried chicken. He loved it. After she left him, he mastered the recipe. Chef Andre Prince Jeffries, Thornton's great-niece, received a James Beard Foundation "American Classics" designation for the now-classic fried chicken dish. Thornton's ex, the true inventor of Nashville Hot Chicken, never got the credit she deserved. Other places in town followed Prince's lead. Soon, the hot style of frying chicken was adopted by Bolton's Spicy Chicken and Fish (founded by Bolton Polk and now operated by his nephew Bolton Matthews), Hattie B's Hot Chicken in Nashville (owned by Nick Bishop Jr. and named for his family's matriarch), Pepperfire Hot Chicken (recently profiled by the *New York Times*), 400 Degrees of Nashville and Deezie's in Murfreesboro. These are the six officially sanctioned Nashville hot chicken providers. The Hot Chicken Coalition, a group of volunteers and civic leaders, has formulated what is required for a dinner to be sanctioned. One of the ingredients must be a pickle. Each of the restaurants uses its own mix of spices and hotness levels. Hattie B's hottest level of heat is called "Shut the Cluck Up."

A separate—but one suspects related—hot fried chicken tradition developed in the Memphis area. Gus' World Famous Hot and Spicy Fried Chicken opened first in Mason, Tennessee, in 1984, and later in Memphis in 2001. Vernon "Gus" Bonner was the son of Napoleon "Na" Vanderbilt and his wife, Miss Maggie. The recipe that Gus used, which his family held in secret since 1953, was the same that his parents had served at their hand-built restaurant on Route 70 outside of Mason. Gus' was discovered by food writers from *Gentleman's Quarterly* and *Saveur*. Gus has a response if anyone should ask for his secret: "This is a dead man's recipe [and] I ain't telling."

Southern fried chicken restaurants abound. New Orleans has two of the best known: Dooky Chase's and Willie Mae's Scotch House, both in the Treme neighborhood. Treme was one of the first residential areas in America established by freed slaves. The rich culinary culture there has African and Afro-Caribbean inspirations—the southern creole tradition. Edgar "Dooky" Chase and his sister Emily opened their restaurant, formerly a sandwich shop, in 1941. Their fried chicken holds the central place on the restaurant's menu. Willie Mae Seton opened her bar, the Scotch House, in 1957. In the early 1970s, and after a move, Willie Mae opened the restaurant, home to some of the best fried chicken in the South.

Any list of the best practitioners of southern fried chicken would have to include Atlanta's Mary Mac's Classic Tea Room (which opened in 1945) and the Colonnade in Buckhead (even older; it opened in 1927). Mrs. Wilke's Dining Room of Savanah opened in the 1940s. Mama Dip (the nickname of Mildred Council) has been serving fried chicken and soul food in Chapel Hill, North Carolina, since the mid-1970s. She was called Mama Dip because she was tall, even as a child, and could reach the dipper into the bottom of a water barrel.

However, the best practitioner of southern fried chicken may be in New York City. Charles Gabriel has been cooking chicken since he was a boy in Raleigh, North Carolina. He moved to New York and cooked at a variety of places and had a food truck until he opened Charles' Southern Style Kitchen in Harlem in the 1990s. It went out of business but reopened in 2009 as Charles' Country Pan-Fried Chicken. As the name implies, Charles does not deep-fry his chicken. He pan-fries it in a gigantic, custom-made cast-iron skillet that can hold twenty to twenty-five pieces of chicken and covers four burners on his stove. It is hand-breaded and not marinated. Charles uses the recipe of his mother, Nora Bell. The *New Yorker* called Charles Gabriel "the Fried-Chicken King of Harlem."

One final note about southern fried chicken: Duncan Hines included four recipes in his book *Adventures in Good Cooking*: two of his own; one from Columbus, Ohio; and one from Indiana. The Indiana recipe came from Mary Fletcher, the cook of writer George Ade, a contemporary of Mark Twain. Hines, once a nationally known figure whose name today is remembered as a brand of cake mix, was a traveling salesman from Bowling Green, Kentucky. He began compiling notes on the places where he found good meals and published his results in his guide. Hines was the first person to publish a guide of good places to eat on the road. His book went through many printings, and he had a syndicated newspaper column. That is how his name came to be associated with cake mix, bread and other baked goods. Hines first discovered Harland Sanders in 1939 and gave Sanders Court and Café a rave review. Subsequent editions of *Adventures* compiled recipes from restaurants Himes particularly enjoyed. His fried chicken recipes seem to follow the Chicken Maryland formula; they are covered and steamed.

Let it be said again that fried chicken is not solely a southern dish. And there are other regional preparations that give southern fried chicken a run for its money. In the Boston area, a restaurant named Ma Glockner's, which opened in 1937, served berched chicken. Berched chicken is first parboiled and then flattened out on a hot grill. In this way it resembles spatchcock, a butterflied and flattened chicken dish. This technique was intended to yield a crisp skin but moist meat. Ma Glockner's closed its doors in 2008, but the River Falls restaurant in Woonsocket, Rhode Island, is now serving the original-recipe berched chicken.

Rhode Island's the Bocce Club, founded in 1930, is also in the Woonsocket area. The Bocce Club was started by the Pavoni family, Italian immigrants, who served chicken roasted—not fried—with pasta. They bought their chickens from Wright's Farm of Harrisville. Gene Wright, the farm's founding owner, was the main supplier of chickens to most of the restaurants in that region. In the early 1950s, he started having barbecues at his farm for local social groups and organizations. These were so popular that Wright decided to open a restaurant on his farm in 1954. The new restaurant, Wright's Farm, featured the same fare as the less formal cookouts. The place was purchased by the Galleshaw family in the 1970s. They expanded the operations to include a gift shop. *Yankee Magazine* honored Wright's with an Editor's Choice Best of New England Award for its family-style chicken dinner. The dinners are chicken, baked, not fried or berched, served with both pasta, as at the Bocce Club, and French fries.

Chicken and waffles is experiencing a wave of popularity, popping up on menus across the country. It sounds as if it was a southern staple, and it probably got its start there. However, the combination of sweet waffles and chicken is popular throughout Pennsylvania and the southwest. In Philadelphia in the early eighteenth century, fried catfish and waffles was a popular menu item. The Pennsylvania Dutch put stewed chicken on top of waffles, and it can be found in homes and restaurants around the state. In the early twentieth century, waffles were used as a bed for many foods, sweet and savory. The fried chicken and waffle dish probably emerged from both African American and Pennsylvania Dutch traditions.

An unusual fried chicken experience can be found in Hamilton on the island of Bermuda. Abdul Hakeem opened Arabian Fried Chicken on a side street not far from the downtown area. Its chicken has a golden, crunchy crust, and the simple preparation is much like Barberton fried chicken.

Barberton fried chicken, it has been said, resembles two dishes from the old Austro-Hungarian Empire, *pohovana piletina* and *wiener backhendl.* The first dish seems to be more Serbian in origin. A YouTube video has Internet chef Ivana Dinulovic preparing the dish. She debones the chicken before breading and frying. The result looks like something a diner would find in Barberton. However, it has no bones. Chicken cooked on the bone has more flavor. Another version of the dish is served with a ketchup-based sauce, nothing like Barberton hot sauce. In Vienna, especially at the open-air Naschmarkt, vendors serve traditional wiener backhendl, which translates roughly to "Viennese breaded fried chicken." This is the nearest thing to the Barberton eating experience you can get.

Jan and Michael Stern wrote about Teibel's in Schererville, Indiana, in two of their books, *Roadfood* and *500 Things to Eat Before You Die.* Grandma

Teibel brought her fried chicken recipe from Vienna. "It is chicken with a crumbly red-gold crust and juicy insides," the Sterns tell us. That makes it sound like both wiener backhendl and Barberton fried chicken. Teibel's was opened in 1929 as a twelve-stool diner by the Teilbel brothers, Martin and Stephen. At the intersection of two highways, Route 30 and Highway 41, the restaurant grew in popularity. It is now in a modern building, almost Frank Lloyd Wright inspired, with several dining rooms, similar to but more elegant than those found at the Barberton fried chicken houses.

Kansas has its famed Chicken Road, near Pittsburg, in the southeast corner of the state. Chicken Annie's and Chicken Mary's are separated only by a tenth of a mile. "Chicken" Annie Frances Rehak went to work at the home of Charles Pichler in 1910. She fell in love with Charles Jr., and the couple married in 1914. Charles went to work in Yale Mining Camp No. 13. In an accident, young Charlie's legs were crushed, and he lost one. White House Chicken was founded for a similar reason, when Mary Marinkovich Pavkov's husband lost his leg. Annie started selling sandwiches and home brew out of her house. She would have Saturday night dinner dances for the other miners and their wives. Eventually, Annie had to expand her home to accommodate all the customers who came by for her food. Her fried chicken cost seventy-five cents for a three-piece dinner—fried chicken, German potato salad, slaw, home-grown pickled peppers, a slice of tomato and bread. Annie raised and prepped her own chickens. Annie and Charlie's son and daughter now operate Chicken Annie's in a larger, modernized restaurant.

Joe and Mary Zerngast opened Chicken Mary's in the 1940s. Joe and Charlie Pichler had worked in the mine together. Joe had a bad heart; like Annie, Mary became the breadwinner. In the beginning, the restaurant had no set hours of operation. Customers would just knock on the door. It was originally called Joe's Place. Cayenne and flat beer go into Mary's fried chicken batter. Perhaps it is a touch of Nashville along the Kansas border. Both restaurants were redone in the '70s. They may have a rivalry going, but after all these years, it must be a friendly one.

The city that challenges Barberton for the best chicken dinners in the Great Lakes is Frankenmuth, Michigan. The quote from Dale Milich that begins this chapter shows how successful the Frankenmuth restaurants are. Zehnder's opened at the Exchange Hotel in 1856. The Zehnder family, William and Emilie Bickel Zehnder, bought the New Exchange Hotel in 1928. They served German-style fried chicken, mashed potatoes, steamed noodles and dressing.

The Bavarian Inn was the Union House Hotel in 1888. It was purchased by Theodore Fischer, who changed the name to Fischer's Hotel. It was Theodore's son Herman and his wife, Lydia, who promoted the Frankenmuth all-you-can-eat chicken dinner concept. Both restaurants seat more than one thousand each. Bavarian Inn servers wear lederhosen and dirndls. Zehnder's has a chicken topiary. There may be a rivalry between Zehnder's and the Bavarian Inn, and it may go deeper than you would think. Elmer Fischer sold out to William "Tiny" Zehnder Jr. in 1959. Both restaurants are now run by cousins (and family feuds are worse than business rivalries).

By the way, these are good German restaurants, serving good German beer. Both restaurants were busted during Prohibition for selling beer.

Closer to home, many chicken houses competed with the Barberton restaurants. The Smithville Inn and Hartville Kitchen are institutions in Northeast Ohio. Both serve Amish family-style dinners of either roasted or fried chicken. The Smithville Inn, less than twenty miles from Barberton, was a stagecoach stop established in 1818. In 1924, it was converted to the restaurant as it is today. It, too, gets its chickens from Gerber's. Hartville Kitchen, founded in 1966, is also about twenty miles away. It serves its own version of hot sauce with its fried chicken. It also serves Jo-Jo potatoes. Jo-Jos are wedges of potato, generally breaded and fried in the same oil as the chicken. There is a possibility that Jo-Jos originated in Ohio, although the name apparently was coined in Minnesota. It was a standard side dish with broasted chicken and is frequently served at pizza shops that also deal in fried chicken.

Many respondents in the Barberton area, when asked to name their favorite fried chicken places, cite pizza shops, especially Rizzi's, Fiesta, Rasicci's and Gionino's. This may be a slap in the face to the Serbian-style chicken houses, but there is no accounting for matters of taste. Many in the area tout the pressure-fried chicken served at Showcase Meats in nearby Kenmore, which opened in 1971. Showcase is a reminder of the old days, when Barbertonians took the streetcar to the Orchard Inn in Kenmore for chicken. Showcase serves its chicken with any number of sides, including Jo-Jos and Barberton hot sauce.

Recently, the email newsletter Thrillist has been touting Krispy Krunchy Chicken as the best chicken chain in America. Krispy Krunchy Chicken is a Louisiana chain founded in 1989. Its menu is comparable to Popeye's, spiced chicken with red beans and rice. The chain has more than 2,300 outlets, mostly in convenience stores and service stations. They have no outlets in or near Barberton. Perhaps they know better.

Chapter Thirteen
BARBERTON TODAY

We Bleed Purple
—Porch sign in Northeast Barberton

William B. Judge, a former city council member, became mayor of Barberton in 2012. His father had been a two-term mayor in the 1980s. Judge, an energetic, enthusiastic man, likes people to call him Bill.

Shortly after his mayoral victory, Judge proposed something that most politicians avoid: a tax hike. Judge spearheaded a .25 percent income tax increase to be used for infrastructure repairs. The city, always a flood risk, needed to create water conservation areas and redo sewer systems. The streets had not been maintained since the city fell on hard times. There were abandoned homes, and the downtown area needed revitalization. Judge has succeeded and easily won his second term.

His Honor is philosophical about industrial cities like his. He knows that the large manufacturing plants will probably not be coming back. Cities may no longer need those large concerns, and small manufacturers and new small businesses can provide a viable economy. But Barberton has something that many similar communities lack: a growing downtown area.

Judge believes that malls killed the downtown shopping area. Now the malls are dying, especially the Rolling Acres Mall outside of Barberton, and downtown shopping districts are coming back. Barberton has the Lake, a state-of-the-art movie theater, and the Magical Theatre Company. The

Tuscarawas Avenue today. *Photo courtesy of the author.*

Snowball Bookshop sits alongside Kave, a coffee shop, and the Nine Muses Art Gallery. *Kave* is the Hungarian word for coffee, and the shop was the idea of students at Barberton High School. When asked what they needed in a downtown area, the students asked for a place to hang out and drink coffee. They had been driving to the Starbucks in Norton. High school students are given a voice in Mayor Judge's administration. A mural on a corner of Second Street proclaims, "From our ancestors came our name, but from our hard work comes our future." The mural was designed by a Barberton High School student.

What a great downtown should offer is walkability and convenience. Barberton now has stores, restaurants, an arts community and the Barberton Public Library. The library has a complete local history area and offers full service to the community. The library is independent of the Akron-Summit County system.

Barberton now has its own brew pub. Ignite Brewery, which pays homage to Barberton's match-making past, is the brainchild of three couples, all of whom are native Barbertonians. Brewmaster Adam Reinhardt and his wife,

The inspirational, student-designed mural on Second Avenue. *Photo courtesy James Carney.*

Marie, serve up beers like Matchstick Blond Ale. The name *Ignite* is a direct nod to sparking activity in an emerging arts district in a once-discounted industrial city.

ACoT (the Art Center on Tuscarawas) is now run by the Akron Area Arts Alliance, which also helmed Akron's Summit Artspace. The Neighborhood Development Services wanted the gallery/studio/learning center to be the cornerstone of the revitalized art and culture district in downtown Barberton. Recently, the city created a walk of fame on Tuscarawas. O.C. Barber and other prominent citizens have memorial tiles embedded along the sidewalk. The walk begins in front of the Lake Theatre, along what is now called the Magic Mile. With new business, restaurants, arts centers and beer, the downtown Barberton shopping area is becoming a magnet, for the young especially.

There are new businesses, but the old keep their traditions alive. The Coffee Pot, a tiny breakfast nook on Second Street Northwest, will celebrate its 100th anniversary in a few years. Minda Ramsey worked there for twenty years before she and her husband, Ken, bought the place. It was founded in

1923 by I.C. Bolin. Although it seats only twenty-four people, the Coffee Pot still serves sixty dozen eggs a week.

Barber's mansion is now Austin Estates, a housing development. A sign on a house near Austin Estates proclaims, "We Bleed Purple," a reference to the colors of Barberton High. Some of the buildings at the Anna Dean Farm are still standing, but shops and offices have been built around it.

Barberton is about adaptability. The venerable Erie Depot on Fourth Street is now an ice cream and sandwich shop. The tiny Neo-Victorian building, erected in 1890 by O.C. Barber, was the conduit for freight, businessmen and factory workers for years. It was a stop on the Erie Railroad line, owned by the New York, Pennsylvania and Ohio Railroad. The depot hosted campaign stops by Presidents William Howard Taft and Theodore Roosevelt. The Liberty Bell passed through, but did not stop, on its way to the Panama Pacific Exposition of 1915. Warren G. Harding's funeral train stopped at the Erie Depot. President Lincoln's funeral train passed through, long before the city had been founded. Kaiser Wilhelm and Czar Nicholas, curious about the secrets of match-making, sent envoys to Barberton. They were met at the depot by the officers of the Diamond Match Company.

Some of the most colorful bits of the Erie Depot's history involve wildlife. In 1914, the first pheasants in Ohio, destined for the Anna Dean Farm, arrived at the depot. In the 1920s, Captain Jonathan Barnett arrived at the Erie Depot with a fifty-five-foot-long, sixty-eight-ton whale named Moby Dick. The exhibit was open twenty-four hours a day, and gawkers learned about whales for twenty-five cents apiece. One grotesque note: the whale had been alive during its travels across our country. Chances are good that it died, finally, in Barberton.

Now the Erie Depot is loved by all in the area for its history as well as for its excellent ice cream. Watched over by a portrait of Charles Mentzer, a stationmaster from a century ago, Gary and Rhonda Ziegenhorn run the place and are proud of the contribution the depot has made to the city. Passenger trains from Akron still bring tourists to town.

Perhaps the biggest boost to the city was the sale of Barberton Citizens Hospital to Summa Health Systems. The hospital was built with money raised by the community. When the sale was finalized in 2007, the city received a large amount of money to be used for education and development. There is about $5 million available annually to schools, which is why the Barberton schools are modern, fully equipped and technology-focused.

As for the four remaining Barberton fried chicken restaurants, business goes on as it has for decades. During the holiday season, when travelers return to the Akron area looking for the dinners they remember, the restaurants had great business. As 2018 began and winter business slowed down, as it tends to do in the north, the restaurateurs looked forward to Valentine's Day, Easter and Mother's Day. Barberton fried chicken goes well with holidays.

Barberton should be known for many things: its industry, its history, its close-knit families, its schools, its burgeoning art scene and, of course, its Serbian fried chicken—an Ohio original.

Afterword

A PERSONAL HISTORY

I was born in Akron in 1952 and have been eating Barberton fried chicken all my life. I was one of those children behind Belgrade Gardens, watching the chickens. My brother Harold said that those chickens would end up as a dinner someday, but I refused to believe him.

Belgrade Gardens was our chicken house of choice, and we dined there almost every Sunday in the summer after swimming at White Pond Beach. White Pond was where my parents met, and where, sixty years later, my brother and I spread some of their cremated remains. Eating at Belgrade Gardens is as much a part of our family lore as White Pond, as much as holiday traditions.

When I was in my teens, and we switched swim clubs to Loyal Oak, we also switched our base of operations to Milich's Village Inn. Sundays would find us in line, eagerly awaiting that golden fried goodness (and the post-dinner Dum Dum). We knew there were other places, but Belgrade and Milich's were our homes away from home.

Things changed in my late teens—an understatement. My best friend Jeff Katz's family went to Terrace Gardens, and they introduced me to the place. I always called it "Terrace Bulba." When we were poor graduate students at the University of Akron, Terrace would be Jeff's and my big splurge dinner. Terrace, you will recall, had the cheapest chicken dinners. Sometimes we would go to Hopocan Gardens. One of the last dinners I had in Akron before moving to Washington, D.C., was at Hopocan Gardens.

My friend Grace Devany Hodges, who may have Barberton roots, always advocated for White House Chicken. I came late to that party but have made up for lost time. (If only they served beer. I like beer with my chicken.) So, I may have been a rarity: someone who dined at all of the Barberton fried chicken places, even though I had a regular home base.

Whenever I returned to Akron, dinner at Barberton was always high on the list of things to do. Barberton and Swenson's hamburgers topped the list. Now that so many loved ones have gone—my parents; Jeff; and my cousin and devoted Belgrade fan Mark—going to one of the chicken houses is a way to connect to my past. My brother said at a recent dinner at Belgrade that it was as if our parents were tucking in with us. This is the underlying reason that I wanted to write this book.

I do not want to get all Marcel Proust, but food, family and memory are all linked. On our first trip to New York, Jeff and I splurged and went to the Russian Tea Room. We ordered expensive and foreign-sounding dishes. When we took our first bite, we looked at each other. "My grandmother used to make this," we said simultaneously.

The History Press posted on Facebook that it was looking for titles for the American Palate series, histories and appreciations of regional foods. My lifelong dream of introducing people to Barberton fried chicken was now a possibility. I have spent time over this past year eating at the chicken houses, reading about the chicken houses and discovering the history of Barberton. Barberton's pride is well deserved. My nostalgia and my love of research combined in writing this book.

I have been fortunate enough to have traveled a bit. Fried chicken speaks a universal language. One afternoon at the Naschmarkt in Vienna, that celebrated open-air collection of produce vendors and food stalls, I sat down to a plate of wiener backhendl, the classic nineteenth-century fried chicken dish. "It's Barberton chicken," I cried. My wife couldn't believe that I wanted to travel halfway across the globe to eat the food of my youth.

BIBLIOGRAPHY

Books

Anderson, Jean. *The American Century Cookbook: The Most Popular Recipes of the 20ᵗʰ Century.* New York: Clarkson Potter, 1997.

Beard, James. *American Cookery.* New York: Little, Brown, 2010.

A Bicentennial Remembrance of Barberton, Ohio, the Magic City. Barberton, OH: Beaumarc Publications, 1975.

Brizova, Joza. *The Czechoslovak Cookbook.* New York: Crown, 1965.

Chamberlain, Lesley. *The Food and Cooking of Eastern Europe.* New York: Penguin, 1989.

Crane, Hart. "Prophyro in Akron." *Complete Poems and Selected Letters.* New York: Library of America, 2006.

Edge, John T. *Fried Chicken: An American Story.* New York: G.P. Putnam's Sons, 2004.

Fleming, William Franklin. *America's Match King: O.C. Barber, 1841–1920.* Barberton, OH: Barberton Historical Society, 1981.

Hagelberg, Kymberli. *Wicked Akron.* Charleston, SC: The History Press, 2010.

Hines, Duncan. *Adventures in Good Eating and the Art of Carving.* Bowling Green, KY: Adventures in Good Eating, 1948.

Kander, Mrs. Simon, and Mrs. Henry Schoenfeld. *The Way to a Man's Heart: The Settlement Cookbook.* Bedford, MA: Applewood Books, 1996.

Kelleher, Stephen E. *Barberton's Very First Cookbook: 125 Years of Culinary Magic.* Barberton, OH: Barberton Historical Society, 2016.

Mariani, John F. *The Encyclopedia of American Food and Drink.* New York: Lebhar-Friedman, 1999.

McKenna, Maryn. *Big Chicken: The Incredible Story of How Antibiotics Created Modern Agriculture and Changed the Way the World Eats.* Washington, D.C.: National Geographic, 2017.

McLagan, Jennifer. *Fat: An Appreciation of a Misunderstood Ingredient, with Recipes.* Berkeley, CA: Ten Speed Press, 2008.

Mitchell, Laurence. *Serbia: The Bradt Travel Guide.* Bucks, UK: Bradt Travel Guides, 2007.

Nathan, John. *Jewish Cooking in America.* New York: Knopf, 1994.

Nealon, Tom. *Food Fights and Culture Wars: A Secret History of Taste.* New York: Overlook Press, 2017.

Pappas, Gregory. *The Magic City: Unemployment in a Working-Class Community.* Ithaca, NY: Cornell University Press, 1989.

Rude, Emelyn. *Tastes Like Chicken: A History of America's Favorite Bird.* New York: Pegasus Books, 2016.

Schrager, Lee Brian. *Fried and True.* New York: Clarkson Potter, 2014.

Smith, Jeff. *The Frugal Gourmet on Our Immigrant Ancestors: Recipes You Should Have Gotten from Your Grandmother.* New York: William Morrow, 1990.

Stern, Jan, and Michael Stern. *500 Things to Eat Before It's Too Late.* Boston: Houghton Mifflin Harcourt, 2009.

———. *Roadfood.* Ninth edition. New York: Clarkson Potter, 2014.

Tannahill, Reay. *Food in History.* NY: Stein and Day, 1973.

Taylor, Phyllis. *100 Years of Magic: The Story of Barberton, Ohio 1891–1991.* Akron, OH: Summit County Historical Society, 1991.

———. *Talk of the Town: Stories from the Barberton Herald April 1891–1991.* Akron, OH: Summit County Historical Society, 1996.

The Third Graders of the O. C. Barber Committee. *The History of Our Magic City: Barberton, Ohio, Founded in 1894.* Barberton City Schools, 2007.

Zibart, Eve, Muriel Stevens and Terrell Vermont. *The Unofficial Guide to Ethnic Cuisine and Dining in America.* New York: Macmillan Travel, 1995.

Articles

Abraham, Lisa. "Belgrade Gardens Celebrating 80 Years." *Akron Beacon Journal,* July 10, 2013.

————. "Pick of the Pecking Order." September 10, 2010.

Barberton Herald. "Original Chicken Houses Celebrate 70 Years." July 10, 2003.

Bloom, Connie. "The New Era: Simple Fare with No Frills." *Akron Beacon Journal,* February 22, 1979.

Brown, Kevin E. "Akron's Eastern European Flavor." *Akron Life and Leisure,* June 2004.

Buford, Bill. "The Secret of Excess." *New Yorker,* August 19, 2002.

Byard, Katie. "Chicken Dynasty to End Long Run." *Akron Beacon Journal,* July 19, 2014.

Canale, Brian. Unpublished history of Hopocan Gardens. Barberton Public Library.

Clark, Meaghan. "The Regional Guide to Fried Chicken." November 1, 2016. www.pastemagazine.com.

Coomes, Jessica. "The End of an Era." *Akron Beacon Journal,* January 12, 2005.

Edge, John T. "The Barberton Birds." *Attaché Magazine* (March 2003).

Giffels, David, "Outsider Tries the Goods." *Akron Beacon Journal,* April 21, 2012.

Girgash, Bill. "Are Your Nerves Frayed? Then Relax with the Fishing Mackos." *Akron Beacon Journal,* June 14, 1953.

Gramlich, Jane. "Seldom Seen: A Forgotten Barberton Neighborhood." *Past Pursuits, Akron-Summit County Public Library Special Collections Newsletter* (Winter 2017).

Halpern, Abby. "United Way Finds Success with Annual Chickenfest." *Barberton Herald,* September 9, 1993.

Hart, Mary Nicklanovich, Milos Papich, Kosta Papich and Sophia Papich. "Belgrade Gardens: Celebrating 80 Years and Three Generations." *Serb World USA* (May/June 2013).

Henry, Dan. "10,000 at Chickenfest to Boost United Way." *Barberton Herald,* September 21, 1989.

Johnson, Eileen. Unpublished history of Terrace Gardens, Barberton Public Library.

Kryza, Andy. "Everything You Need to Know About Fried Chicken." Thrillist.com, January 2, 2014.

Kuher, Patti. "It's Chickenfest! Weekend in the Chicken Capital." *Barberton Herald,* September 5, 1991.

Louie, Andre. "Finger-Lickin', Knee-Slappin' Fun." *Akron Beacon Journal,* September 17, 1988.

Milich, Dale. Unpublished history of Milich's Village Inn. Barberton Public Library, December 10, 1978.

Muller, Robert. "Iron Chef Chooses Belgrades." *Barberton Herald*, September 16, 2010.

Murphey, Francis B. "Go Ahead—Chicken Out in Barberton." *Akron Beacon Journal*, May 4, 1988.

Nichols, Kenneth. "Town Crier: A Dog's Life Hardly Compares to a Chicken." *Akron Beacon Journal*, November 18, 1969.

Papich, Sophia Topalsky, "How Did a Little Farmhouse Restaurant in Barberton, Ohio Gain a Worldwide Reputation for Great Chicken Dinners?" Unpublished history.

Patterson, Ruth. "Making the Rounds with the Gaddy Gourmet." *Akron Beacon Journal*, February 6 , 1956.

Pavkov, Al. Unpublished history of White House Chicken, Barberton Public Library, December 10, 1978.

Peacock, Nancy. "In the Land of the Chicken People." *Akron Beacon Journal Magazine*, December 10, 1978.

Prero, Mike. "The Story of a Giant: Diamond Match Company, 1881–Present." *Hobby History* (July/August 1997).

Price, Mark J. "Yum: Kids Got 1ˢᵗ Taste of Dum-Dums." *Akron Beacon Journal*, October 23, 2017.

Schleis, Lisa. "Barberton Discovers Magic of Chicken. "*Akron Beacon Journal*, January 4, 1997.

———. "Barberton Legacy Dims a Bit: Terrace Gardens Closes Shop." *Akron Beacon Journal*, January 4, 1997.

———. "Petticoat Thief Lives." *Akron Beacon Journal*, October 18, 2002.

Shaffer, Chef Bev. "Fanning the Flames of Food Rivalry." *Akron Art and Leisure* (December 2010).

Simonds, Jack. "Barbertonians Agree: Chickenfest! Is Plucky." *Barberton Herald*, September 13, 1988.

Snow, Jane. "A Deep-Fried Secret." *Akron Beacon Journal*, November 2, 1988.

———. "German Eatery Gives Up the Ghost. Continuing Roadwork Cripples Business." *Akron Beacon Journal*, September 30, 1994.

———. "How I Cracked the Case: When the Chickens Weren't Talking and the Stool Pigeons Couldn't Be Bought." *Akron Beacon Journal*.

Spitz, Kathleen. "The New Era Serves Up a Lot for a Little." *Akron Beacon Journal*, January 22, 1988.

Unger, Diane. "Barberton Fried Chicken." *Cook's Country Magazine* (June–July 2011).

Vargo, Karen. "Area United Way Kicks Off Campaign with 5th Annual 'Thanks' to Contributors." *Barberton Herald*, 1992.

Warner, Stuart. "It's Chickenfest Time, Lame Yolks and All." *Akron Beacon Journal*, September 15, 1989.

Webb, Craig. "Barberton Chicken Belittled?" *Akron Beacon Journal*, April 15, 2002.

Television Programs

"American Feuds." *Food Feuds*. Food Network. November 4, 2010.

Websites

Barberton Historical Society. http://www.annadeanfarm.com/construct. htm.

Bolois, Jason. "17 Bucket-List Fried Chicken Restaurants to Try Before You Die." First We Feast. February 11, 2015. http://www.firstwefeast.com.

Buie, Lisa. "Magic City Chicken Tour." YouTube. April 14, 2017. www. youtube.com.

Canale, Brian. "White House Chicken Food Feuds" (interview). YouTube. https://www.youtube.com/watch?v=5aVt5WxgtlQ.

City of Barberton. "Barberton History." http://cityofbarberton.com/oc/ history.shtml.

Kubilius, Kerry. "Traditional Foods to Try in Eastern Europe." Trip Savvy. June 14, 2017. www.tripsavvy.com.

Minyungee. "Eastern European Food. What Is It, Really?" You Eatin' Nice. February 19, 2012. https://minyungee.wordpress.com.

National Cleveland-Style Polka Hall of Fame. http://www.clevelandstyle. com/frankie~spetich.html.

Noe, Tom. Exploring Food My Way. exploringfoodmyway.blogspot.com.

Productions427. "De-Vore vs Evil Meals." YouTube. July 7, 2011. www. youtube.com.

Queen City Sausage. http://www.queencitysausage.com.

Russian Tea Room. http://www.russiantearoomnyc.com/about-us.

Wikimedia. Various articles.

Wikipedia. Various articles.

INDEX

K

KFC 103

M

Macko's 17, 91, 92, 93, 94, 95
Mijo's House of Paprikash 49
Milich's Village Inn 11, 17, 56, 62,
        71, 84, 85, 87, 89, 90, 97, 115

N

New Era, the 49

O

Ohio and Erie Canal 23

P

Popeye's 103, 108
Pramuka, Albert V. 44

V

Village Inn 17, 53, 77, 85, 87, 88,
        89, 90

W

White House Chicken 11, 17, 25,
        53, 54, 56, 61, 69, 72, 75, 76,
        77, 78, 79, 81, 82, 87, 89, 94,
        103, 107, 116

ABOUT THE AUTHOR

 **R**onald Koltnow is a retired sales representative for Penguin Random House. He has been a consultant for Your Expert Nation, a supervisor at Blue Cross and Blue Shield and a bookseller. Koltnow's articles have appeared in the *AARSC Journal*, *Magill's Survey of Cinema*, *Magill's Film Annual* and Washington, D.C.'s *City Paper*. He is a native Akronite but currently resides in Boston with his wife and two beloved cats.

Visit us at
www.historypress.com